The Money Machine
How the City Works

FIFTH EDITION

Philip Coggan

PENGUIN BOOKS

PENGUIN BOOKS

Penguin Books Ltd, 80 Strand, London WC2R ORL, England
Penguin Putnam Inc., 375 Hudson Street, New York, New York 10014, USA
Penguin Books Australia Ltd, 250 Camberwell Road, Camberwell, Victoria 3124, Australia
Penguin Books Canada Ltd, 10 Alcorn Avenue, Toronto, Ontario, Canada M4V 3B2
Penguin Books India (P) Ltd, 11, Community Centre, Panchsheel Park, New Delhi – 110 017, India
Penguin Books (NZ) Ltd, Cnr Rosedale and Airborne Roads, Albany, Auckland, New Zealand
Penguin Books (South Africa) (Pty) Ltd, 24 Sturdee Avenue, Rosebank 2196, South Africa

Penguin Books Ltd, Registered Offices: 80 Strand, London WC2R ORL, England

www.penguin.com

Published in Penguin Books 1986
Second edition 1989
Third edition 1995
Fourth edition 1999
Fifth edition 2002

9

Copyright © Philip Coggan, 1986, 1989, 1995, 1999, 2002

The moral right of the author has been asserted

Set in 9.5/12 pt Adobe Minion
Typeset by Rowland Phototypesetting Ltd, Bury St Edmunds, Suffolk
Printed in England by Clays Ltd, St Ives plc

ISBN-13: 978–0–141–00930–8

Contents

Acknowledgements

A book covering such a wide field could not be produced without the help and advice of many people. First and foremost, I would like to thank Nick Shepherd and Diane Pengelly for reading through all the chapters and pointing out the numerous grammatical errors and nonsensical statements. Many others read through individual chapters: my father, Ken Ferris, John Presland, David Bowen, Clifford German, Paul and Vanessa Gilbert, Lynton Jones, David Morrison and Nigel Falls, and I thank them for their helpful comments. Jeremy Stone made many useful points about the structure and the contents of the book. All mistakes are, of course, mine and not theirs. A distinguished mention should be given to Mr Alan Michael Sugar for bringing out his Amstrad word-processor at just the right time and price to allow me to benefit. Last but not least, I thank Churchy for all the help in typing and for putting up with the sight of my back as I slaved away on the manuscript.

P.C.
March 1986

ACKNOWLEDGEMENTS TO FOURTH AND FIFTH EDITIONS

The City changes so fast these days that it is hard work keeping up. I would like to thank my colleagues at the *Financial Times* for their immense knowledge and expertise. And most of all, my wife Sandie, whose love and support have changed my life.

P.C.
May 2002

Introduction

People are becoming much more interested in finance. For some, the motivation is simple: they have come to realize that the stock market provides an opportunity for making easy money or, at least, a comfortable nest egg for retirement. For others, the feeling is far more antagonistic. They see the financial markets as part of a sinister conspiracy, including multinational corporations and institutions like the International Monetary Fund, that controls the world and imposes free market dogma on unwilling populations.

This ambivalent attitude towards financiers dates back over centuries. Roman emperors and medieval monarchs had to flatter financiers when they needed to borrow money; the attitude quickly turned to revulsion when the time came to pay it back. Whole populations have been caught up in frenzies of speculation dating back from Dutch tulip mania through the South Sea Bubble to the Florida land boom of the 1920s. Individual financiers have found it laughably easy to buy popularity when their schemes were prospering (think of Robert Maxwell). But there have been no shortages of commentators saying 'I told you so' when their empires subsequently collapsed.

Perhaps the public has tended to treat the subject of finance as a soap opera (complete with heroes and villains) because too few people attempt to understand the workings of the financial system. Although the details of individual financial deals can be very complex, there are basic principles in finance which everyone can understand and which apply as much to the finances of Mr Smith, the grocer, as to Barclays Bank. The more fully people understand these principles, the more they will be able and willing to criticize, and perhaps even participate in, the workings of the financial system. Like all areas of public life, it needs criticism to ensure its efficiency.

Even those who do not own shares should care about how the City performs. It is one of the UK's biggest industries and a vital overseas earner in areas such as insurance and fund management.

THE CITY

First of all, what is the role of the UK financial system, and in particular of the City of London, which is at its heart?

Its primary function is to put people who want to lend (invest) in touch with people who want to borrow. A simple example of this role is that of the building societies. They collect the small savings of individuals and lend them to house buyers who want mortgages.

Why do the savers not just lend directly to borrowers, without the intervention of financial institutions? The main reason is that their needs are not compatible with those of the end borrowers. People with mortgages, for example, want to borrow for at least twenty-five years. Savers may want to withdraw their money next week. In addition, the amounts needed are dissimilar. Companies and governments need to borrow amounts far beyond the resources of most individuals. Only by bundling together all the savings of many individuals can the financial institutions provide funds on an appropriate scale.

Who are the borrowers? One prominent set is industrial companies. Companies will always need money to pay for raw materials, buildings, machinery and wages before they can generate their own revenues by selling their goods or services. To cover the period before the cash flows in, companies either borrow from the banks or raise capital in the form of shares or bonds. Without this capital it would be impossible for companies to invest and for the economy to expand.

The second major set of borrowers is governments. No matter what their claims to fiscal rectitude, few governments have ever managed to avoid spending more than they receive. The UK government and other nations' governments come to the City to cover the difference.

Who wants to lend? In general, the only part of the economy which is a net saver (i.e. its savings are greater than its borrowings) is the personal sector – individuals like you and me. Rarely do we lend directly to the government or industry or other individuals: instead we save, either through the medium of banks and building societies or, in a more planned way, through pension and life assurance schemes. Lending, saving and investing are thus different ways of looking at the same activity.

So financial institutions are there to channel the funds of those who want to lend into the hands of those who want to borrow. They take their cut as middle-men. That cut can come in two forms: banks can charge a higher interest rate to the people to whom they lend than they pay to the people from whom they borrow, or they can simply charge a fee for bringing lender and borrower, or issuer and investor, together.

There is no doubt that financial institutions perform an immensely valuable service: imagine life without cheque books, cashpoint cards, mortgages and hire-purchase agreements. Even those Britons who do not have a bank account would never be paid if the companies for which they work did not have one. Indeed, the companies might not have been founded without loans from banks.

It is important, when considering some of the practices discussed in this book, to remember that the business of financial institutions is the handling of money. Some of their more esoteric activities, like financial futures, can appear to the observer to be mere speculation. But speculation is an unavoidable part of the world of financial institutions. They must speculate, when they borrow at one rate, that they will be able to lend at a higher rate. They must speculate that the companies to whom they lend will not go bust. To criticize the mechanisms by which they do speculate is to ignore the basic facts of financial life.

Financial institutions are a vital part of the British economy. Whether the rewards they receive are in keeping with the importance of the part they play is another question, which we will examine in the final chapter.

THE INSTITUTIONS

The most prominent financial institutions are the banks, which can be divided roughly into two groups, commercial (retail) and investment (merchant) banks. The former rely on the deposits drawn from ordinary individuals, on which they pay little or no interest and which they re-lend at a profit. Commercial banks must ensure that they have enough money to repay their customers, so their investments tend to be short term. The latter group relies more on fees earned from arranging deals such as takeovers and captial-raising issues. Nowadays many commercial banks have investment banking arms; the two are intertwined.

The second group of financial institutions, known as the investment institutions, include the pension funds and life insurance companies. They bundle together the monthly savings of individuals and invest them in a range of assets, including the shares of British and foreign companies and commercial property. This is a vital function, since industry needs long-term funds to expand. Banks lend money to industry, but by tradition they have been less ready to lend for long periods. Pension funds can count on regular contributions and can normally calculate in advance when and how much they will have to pay out to claimants. Life insurance companies have the laws of actuarial probabilities to help them calculate their likely outgoings.

The third main group is the exchanges, which provide a market for trading in the capital that companies and governments have raised. People and institutions are more willing to invest money in tradeable instruments, since they can easily reclaim their money if the need arises. The best-known exchange in the UK is the Stock Exchange.

Within and outside these groups is a host of institutions which perform specialized functions. The building societies have already been mentioned, but we will also need to look at the Bank of England, insurance brokers and underwriters, to name but a few.

THE INSTRUMENTS

Chapter 2 examines in detail questions about the definition of money and the determination of interest rates. But for the moment the best way to understand the workings of the financial system is to stop thinking of money as a homogeneous commodity and instead to think of notes and coins as constituting one of a range of financial assets. It is the *liquidity* of those assets that distinguishes them from each other. The liquidity of an asset is judged by the speed with which it can be exchanged for goods without financial loss.

Notes and coins are easily the most liquid because they can be traded immediately for goods. At the opposite extreme is a long-term loan, which may not be repaid for twenty-five years. Between the two extremes are various financial assets which have grown up in response to the needs of the individuals and institutions that take part in the financial markets.

Essentially, financial assets can be divided into three types: *loans*, *bonds* and *equities*.

Loans are the simplest to understand. One party agrees to lend another money in return for a payment called *interest*, normally quoted as an annual rate. It is possible, as in the case of many mortgages or hire-purchase agreements, for the principal sum (that is, the original amount borrowed) to be paid back in instalments with the interest. Alternatively, the principal sum can be paid back in one lump at the end of the agreed term.

Bonds are pieces of paper like IOUs, which borrowers issue in return for a loan and which are bought by investors, who can sell them to other parties as and when they choose. Bonds are normally medium- to long-term (between five and twenty-five years) in duration. The period for which a loan or bond lasts is normally known as its *maturity*, and the interest rate a bond pays is called the *coupon*. Shorter-term bonds (lasting three months or so) are generally known as *bills*.

Equities are issued only by companies and offer a share in the assets and profits of the firm, which has led to their being given the more common name of *shares*. They differ from other financial instruments in that they confer ownership of something more than just a piece of paper. In the financial sense, shareholders *are* the company, whereas bondholders are merely outside creditors.

The initial capital invested in shares will rarely be repaid unless the company folds up. (But shares, like bonds, can be sold to other investors.) The company will generally announce a semi-annual dividend (a sum payable to each shareholder as a proportion of the profit), depending on the size of its profits. All ordinary shareholders will receive that dividend. However, it is not compulsory for companies to pay dividends. Some companies choose not to do so because they wish to reinvest all their profits with the aim of expanding the business. Others may omit paying a dividend because they are in financial difficulties.

Equity investors only get paid after the demands of lenders and bond-holders are satisfied. If a company gets into trouble, equity investors may well lose the bulk of their money whereas bondholders have a chance of getting a chunk of their capital back. The good news for equity investors is they get all the upside. Whereas the claims of lenders and bondholders are fixed, equity owners benefit from a company's growth.

That brings us to one of the most important principles in finance. *Greater risk demands greater reward.* If a lender is dubious about whether a borrower will be able to repay the loan, he or she will charge a higher rate on that loan. Why lend money at 10 per cent to a bad risk when you can lend money at 10 per cent to a good risk and be sure that your money will be returned with interest? To compensate for the extra risk, you will demand a rate of, say, 12 per cent, for the borrower with a doubtful reputation.

ALCHEMY

Financial institutions must perform a feat of alchemy. They must transform the cash savings of ordinary depositors, who may want to withdraw their money at any moment, into funds which industry can borrow for twenty-five years or more. This process involves risk – the risk that the funds will be withdrawn before the institutions' investments mature. They must therefore demand a higher return for tying up their money for long periods, so that they can offset that risk. This brings us to a second important principle of finance. *Lesser liquidity demands greater reward.* The longer an investor must hold an asset before being sure of achieving a return, the larger he will expect that return to be. However, this is not an iron rule. In Chapter 2 we shall see how, for a variety of reasons, long-term interest rates can be below short-term rates.

The range of financial assets extends from cash to long-term loans. Cash, the most liquid of assets, gives no return at all. A building society account that can be withdrawn without notice might give a return of, say, 5 per cent. In the circumstances, why should lenders make a twenty-five-year loan at less than 5 per cent? They would be incurring an unnecessary risk for no reward. So lenders generally demand a greater return to compensate them for locking up their money for a long period. In the same way some banks and building societies offer higher-interest accounts to those who agree to give ninety days' notice before withdrawal.

The borrowers (in this case, the banks and building societies) are willing to pay more for the certainty of retaining the funds.

Bonds and shares are usually liquid in the sense that they can be sold, but the seller has no guarantee of the price that he or she will receive for them. This differentiates them from savings accounts, which guarantee the return of the capital invested. Thus bond- and shareholders will generally demand a higher return. For both, that extra return may come through an increase in the price of the investment rather than through a high interest rate or dividend. This applies especially to shares. As a consequence, the dividends paid on shares is often, in percentage terms, well below the interest paid on bonds such as gilts (highly reliable investments because they are issued by the UK government).

There is another group of financial instruments, which confers the right to buy or sell another instrument. In this category are options, futures and warrants. They allow two important activities, *hedging* and *leverage*.

Hedging is the process whereby an institution buys or sells a financial instrument in order to offset the risk that the price of another financial instrument or commodity may rise or fall. For example, coffee importers buy coffee futures to lock in the cost of their raw materials and reduce the risk that a rise in commodity prices will cut their profits.

Leverage gives the investor an opportunity for a large profit with a small stake. Options, futures and warrants all provide the chance of leverage because their prices vary more sharply than those of the underlying commodities to which they are linked. These concepts are more fully explained in Chapters 12 and 13.

THE CITY'S INTERNATIONAL ROLE

The City, of course, plays a role that far exceeds the dimensions of the national economy. It is this role that the supporters of the City invoke when they defend its actions and its privileges. And it is to preserve this role that the City has undergone so many changes in recent years.

In the nineteenth century the City's importance in the world financial markets reflected the way in which Britannia ruled the waves. Britain financed the development of Argentinian and North American railways, for example. By 1914 Britain owned an enormous range of foreign assets, which brought it a steady overseas income. Much of the world's trade was conducted in sterling because it was a respected and valued currency.

The two world wars ended Britain's financial predominance. Foreign assets were repatriated to pay for the fighting. As the Empire disintegrated, so too did the world's use of sterling as a trading instrument. Just as the USA emerged as the world's biggest economic power, so New York challenged London for the market in financial services and the dollar took over from sterling as the major trading currency. It seemed that Britain and the City would become backwaters on the edge of Europe.

One thing saved the City. The USA, which had regarded banks with suspicion since the Great Crash of 1929, did not welcome the growth of New York as a financial centre. The US authorities began to place restrictions on the activities of its banks and investors. International business began to flow back to London, where there were fewer restrictions. The Euromarket (see Chapter 10) grew into the most important capital market in the world and made London its base.

The revival of the City in the 1960s brought many foreign banks to London and they have stayed as Britain's capital has become one of the world's three great trading centres, together with New York and Tokyo. But the challenge is never-ending. The development of the European single currency may mean that London could lose its place to Paris or Frankfurt.

The London Stock Exchange has already made an abortive attempt to merge with Frankfurt and many believe that a single European exchange is inevitable in the long term. Indeed, some believe that the world's multinational companies will eventually be traded on a single global electronic exchange.

It is best that we look at these changes before we examine in detail the workings of the UK financial system. Discussion of these changes requires an assumption of some knowledge on the part of the reader as to how the system works. However, this book is also designed to be read by those who know little of finance. They may well want to start at Chapter 2 and return to the first chapter after they have read the rest.

1   The International Financial Revolution

In the past thirty years, the City has been changed beyond recognition. It has always been an important part of the UK economy and a key source of overseas earnings, particularly in areas such as banking and insurance.

The City, or at least its financial markets, has always been powerful. Many blame a 'bankers' ramp' for forcing out the Labour government in 1931, and subsequent Labour governments ran into problems over sterling in 1948, 1967 and 1976. But now the financial markets' influence seems all-pervasive. Governments round the world find themselves constrained in their economic policies for fear of offending the markets. James Carville, one of President Clinton's key advisers, remarked that he would like to be reincarnated as the bond market so he could 'intimidate everybody'. A combination of lower tax rates and liberalized financial markets has widened income differentials. Many City employees earn as much in a year as normal people might hope to earn in a lifetime, helping to force the prices of properties in London beyond the reach of teachers and doctors.

Wider share ownership, encouraged by the government through privatizations and tax breaks, has created much greater interest in financial markets, reflected in greater coverage in newspapers and on TV. And, with governments round the world quailing in the face of the cost of state pension schemes, citizens are realizing that they may depend on the financial markets for their security in old age.

Why has all this happened? In part, it is because of the breakdown of the financial system that prevailed from the end of the Second World War until the early 1970s. That system, generally known as Bretton Woods, combined fixed exchange rates with strict controls on capital flows, so restricting the scope for financial market activity. Under fixed exchange rates, currency speculation was only profitable at occasional times, such as when Britain was forced to devalue sterling in 1967.

Foreign-exchange controls also made it difficult for investors to buy equities outside their home markets. That reduced the scope for share trading and ensured that the UK equity market was a protected haven, dominated by small firms operating in a climate which author Philip Augar has described as 'gentlemanly capitalism'.

But the system broke down in the early 1970s (for a full description see Chapter 13). The first domino to fall was fixed exchange rates. The system had depended on the US dollar but that currency buckled in the face of the costs of the Vietnam War.

Once exchange rates began to float, two things started to happen. First, companies faced foreign-exchange risk when selling goods. For example, Mercedes' costs were in Deutschmarks; when it sold a car in the US, it received dollars. If the dollar fell against the Deutschmark, that would be bad news. So companies looked for ways to protect themselves from these risks.

Secondly, floating exchange rates created the potential for continuous speculation. The 1970s saw the creation of the financial futures market in Chicago, which allowed traders to bet on the likely movement of exchange rates.

Both developments were opportunities for the financial system. They could make money speculating on the markets and they could make money helping companies protect themselves from foreign-exchange risk. Both opportunities were taken.

Floating exchange rates also had significant implications for governments. Think of three key elements of monetary policy: exchange rates, interest rates and capital controls. Under the Bretton Woods system, countries controlled their exchange rates and capital flows. However, if countries ran a substantial trade deficit, capital would still flow out of the country.

Take the UK, a country which habitually runs a trade deficit. When a foreign company sells goods to the UK, it receives sterling in return. (Even if it asks for dollars, the UK buyer of the goods must sell sterling and buy dollars in order to make the payment. Sterling will still flow out of the country.) Eventually, those companies will become less and less willing to hold sterling at the prevailing exchange rate. The Bank of

England may be willing to buy that sterling off the overseas companies but it needs foreign-exchange reserves to do so. After a while the money will run out.

To avoid this problem, governments tried to cut the trade deficit. The easiest way of doing so was to raise interest rates; this had the effect of cutting consumer demand for foreign goods. But the result was a stop-go kind of economy, in which periods of rapid expansion were suddenly cut short as governments raised interest rates to protect sterling.

In a world of floating exchange rates, there is no requirement for governments to ratchet up interest rates every time the currency falls. Voters naturally don't like high interest rates. The problem was exacerbated by governments' desire to keep unemployment low; at the slightest sign of economic weakness, they acted to boost the economy.

So in the 1970s, governments let their currencies sag, and kept interest rates lower than they might have been. The result (higher import prices, too much money chasing too few goods) was inflation. By the end of the 1970s, there was a general feeling that the old system of economic policy had failed. Governments had tried to micro-manage the economy but in their attempts to keep down unemployment, they had merely achieved stagflation: high inflation and unemployment. Right-wing politicians such as Ronald Reagan and Margaret Thatcher argued that state intervention in industry had stifled the economy, concentrating resources in sunset industries such as coal and steel, and starving the growth sectors of the economy such as technology.

Inflation was eventually brought to heel with the help of very high interest rates, which also prompted massive job losses in those sunset industries. This process caused much distress and protest at the time and would have been politically impossible without the economic chaos of the 1970s.

At the same time (and to rather less fanfare), governments in the US and the UK relaxed the regulations on the financial sector and abolished capital controls. The idea was that the economy would function best when the markets, rather than bureaucrats, decided where to allocate capital.

Suddenly, investors were free to invest anywhere in the globe. Instead of concentrating on old UK stalwarts such as Imperial Chemical Industries or Marks & Spencer, they were free to invest in the likes of Bayer of Germany or Wal-Mart of the US.

These changes had enormous consequences for those who traded shares in the City. The old system had been like a gentlemen's club. A group of people called jobbers did all the trading in shares. They were not allowed to deal directly with investors. Instead, a group of intermediaries called brokers linked investors and jobbers, finding the best prices for the former in return for a fixed commission.

In theory, this system protected the interests of investors. Because brokers did not trade in shares, they could give independent advice to investors. And because brokers could shop around, jobbers had to offer competitive prices.

But there were two problems with this system. The first was that it was clearly not a free market: jobbers and brokers were restricted in the role they could play and commissions were fixed. Brokers could not compete on price.

The second was that the broking and jobbing firms were all small. This was fine in a world where equity trading was limited to the home market. But when investment became international, the domestic firms were just too small to cope; they did not have the capital to deal with the risks involved.

BIG BANG

The solution was Big Bang: a set of sweeping changes that were implemented in 1986. The old distinction between brokers and jobbers was abolished – firms could both act for investors and trade in shares. Outside capital was brought in, with UK, European and US banks buying up existing broking and jobbing firms.

A whole generation of senior brokers and jobbers retired on the proceeds of the sales and famous names such as de Zoete & Bevan, or Akroyd & Smithers, either disappeared or were subsumed within larger groups. (The process is well described in *The Death of Gentlemanly Capitalism* by Philip Augar, published by Penguin.) The old Stock Exchange floor, where brokers and jobbers met face to face, became a museum piece. Now the bulk of the trading was done by telephone, with investors kept constantly updated on share prices by brightly coloured

Topic computer screens – with red signalling a falling price and blue, a rising one.

The whole process brought benefits to institutional investors, since the abolition of fixed commissions substantially cut their trading costs. But it had its downsides as well. One substantial problem was that the integration of broking and trading created an automatic conflict of interest within the financial sector. When a broker recommended a stock, was that because of a genuine opinion or because the trading arm of his firm had a large position in the shares? In recent years, a more significant conflict of interest has arisen. The abolition of fixed commissions has gradually ensured that commissions are only a small part of any bank's revenues. But, in theory, institutional investors are supposed to reward analysts by placing trades with the firms concerned. The sums do not add up.

Instead, banks have concentrated on increasing their revenues from transaction fees – acting for corporations in issuing new shares or bonds and making takeovers. This has led to analysts becoming 'cheerleaders' for such companies, talking up their prospects so that the deals will be successful. The idea of thoughtful, unbiased research has been severely compromised.

The second problem that followed Big Bang was that control of equity trading moved out of the hands of UK institutions. It was inevitable that control of part of the City would move overseas: the US, European and Japanese banks all had a lot of capital. But it seemed for a while as if the UK could develop domestic champions. One such was Barclays, which bought the broker de Zoete & Bevan, and the jobber Wedd Durlacher, and created BZW. Another was SG Warburg, a successful merchant bank that bought brokers Rowe & Pitman, Mullens, and the jobber Akroyd & Smithers.

Alas, all the UK champions eventually dropped out of the race. This development was prompted by the next stage of the international financial revolution, which occurred during the 1990s.

THE END OF THE COLD WAR

Free-market philosophy may have swept the board in the US and the UK during the 1980s but it was not so successful elsewhere. Many observers believed that this so-called Anglo-Saxon model was inferior to those developed elsewhere, particularly in Germany and Japan.

Both countries decided against giving the markets free rein. In Germany, hostile corporate takeovers were virtually unknown: companies had close relationships with their banks, which had seats on the boards. Maximizing returns to shareholders was not the priority it was in the Anglo-Saxon system; instead the interests of customers, suppliers and employees were taken into account.

In Japan, takeovers were also unknown. Companies were protected against them by elaborate cross-shareholding with friendly groups. Maximizing profits was seen as less important to Japanese managers than maximizing sales and market share.

To their admirers, the German and Japanese systems seemed to offer many advantages. The absence of takeovers allowed companies to plan for the future, regardless of short-term profit performance. The result was higher investment. And the focus on employees seemed far less socially divisive than the Anglo-Saxon model.

Under the German-Japanese models, the freedom of financial markets played second fiddle to other factors. That did not stop the Japanese stock market soaring to unprecedented heights in the late 1980s.

Of course, until the end of the Cold War, a large part of the world followed a communist or socialist-style model, in which the financial markets played virtually no role at all.

All this changed during the course of the 1990s. The collapse of communism was clearly an epochal event and appeared to underline that there was no alternative to capitalism as an economic model. Suddenly a whole raft of countries moved into the Western economic system, adopting stock markets and allowing US companies like McDonald's to open for business.

The collapse of communism also led to the reunification of Germany. The immense costs involved in taking on the old East Germany led to the imposition of high interest rates by the Bundesbank, the German central bank, in an attempt to control inflationary pressures. (This also eventually led to the break up of the Exchange Rate Mechanism.) By the mid 1990s, the German model no longer looked so attractive. German unemployment was far higher than that prevailing in the US. German social costs were also far higher, prompting some German companies to site facilities overseas. German politicians began to feel that high taxes were deterring entrepreneurship and causing sluggish economic growth. An ageing German population suggested that, in the long run, pension costs could become a massive burden on the German state.

So, slowly but surely, Germany and the rest of Europe started to edge towards the Anglo-Saxon model. Businesses began to talk of 'shareholder value'; they divested themselves of non-core operations, simplified their shareholding structures and focused on improving profits. Perhaps the ultimate signal of the change in culture came in early 2000 when Mannesmann of Germany was taken over by Vodafone of the UK; this in a culture where hostile takeovers were extremely rare, let alone a hostile takeover by a foreign company.

As Germany moved in an Anglo-Saxon direction, the attractions of the Japanese model also faded. In the late 1980s, Japan's economy developed all the symptoms of a speculative bubble: share prices rose to record levels in terms of profits or dividends while land prices also soared.

The bubble popped in 1990 and some of Japan's apparent virtues began to be revealed as vices. Companies did not worry about short-term profits, but this led them to invest in unsuitable projects. The absence of takeovers meant there was no market discipline on poor companies to perform well. The soaring stock market also led companies to indulge in speculation which proved ill-timed once the market turned. The friendly relationship between banks and the corporate sector meant that the banks were saddled with bad loans, a problem that has still not been sorted out.

Japan spent much of the 1990s stuck in a deflationary trap. Despite a host of government spending packages and interest rates that eventually fell to zero, the Japanese authorities found no way of reviving their economy.

The problems of Japan caused an almost 180-degree turn in the commentaries of those writing about economics and management. In the late 1980s, bestselling books were written about how the US should copy the Japanese; by the late 1990s, there was almost unanimous agreement on the need for all countries to copy the US.

THE US ECONOMIC MIRACLE

The retreat from the German and Japanese models was not just about their perceived failures; it was also about the perceived success of the US.

By the late 1990s, the US seemed by far the most dynamic of the world's economies. Growth averaged more than 4 per cent a year, and that growth was achieved with barely a trace of inflation. At the same time, European economies struggled to grow at 2–3 per cent a year; the Japanese economy struggled to grow at all. Unemployment fell to 4–5 per cent, around half the level prevailing in Europe. There was, apparently, a productivity miracle (the figures were subsequently revised down but still showed a substantial improvement over the 1980s).

In almost every growth industry – software, hardware, the Internet, biotechnology, media – the US appeared to lead the world. The US accordingly attracted floods of capital from overseas; both the dollar and the US stock market rose substantially.

Economists attributed the US success to the openness of its economy, the lack of regulations, the use of share options to motivate executives and employees, and a host of other 'free market' factors. Understandably, countries trying to emulate the US example tended to adopt some of those measures.

Free-market enthusiasts also pointed to the success of those Asian countries that had followed a broadly free-market view, such as Singapore, Hong Kong and Taiwan, and the failure of those countries, notably in Africa, that had followed a statist or socialist model.

A so-called 'Washington consensus' argued that any economy which wanted to prosper should follow the free-market model: lower taxes, reducing government deficits and open capital markets. These policies were often made a condition for countries requiring aid from the International Monetary Fund, the Washington-based organization that underpins the global financial system.

Such policies were sometimes deeply controversial. Usually, countries only turn to the IMF for help when their economies are in recession; in such circumstances, cutting government deficits can make matters worse in the short term. Spending cuts usually have the heaviest impact on the poor.

The anti-globalization protests that have taken place over the last few years cite IMF policies as one of their targets. They also argue that the World Trade Organization, a body which settles trade disputes between countries, 'imposes' free-market dogma on countries and fails to allow for social and environmental concerns.

GLOBALIZATION

What is globalization? It is one of those terms that is often used, but more rarely defined. Broadly speaking, it is a trend whereby trade, investment and culture have become ever more international.

What we have defined we can attempt to measure. Is globalization new? Not in terms of trade. In the UK, exports formed 29.8 per cent of GDP back in 1913: in 2000, they were just 20.7 per cent. Other countries are more open to trade than they were before the First World War but arguably, in this respect, the modern economy is not that much different from the one familiar to the Edwardians. It was the opening up of the US prairie states, and the consequent arrival of cheap wheat, that devastated British agriculture in the late nineteenth century.

Globalization has taken a backward step in terms of population movements. The immigration rate to the US peaked at 10.4 per cent of the population in 1910; in 1990, it was just 2.6 per cent.

In terms of trade and population movements, the world was pretty 'globalized' before the First World War; the subsequent battles with fascism and communism sent that process into reverse for sixty years.

In two respects, however, globalization has surpassed the First World War system. In terms of investment, ownership of foreign assets peaked as a proportion of world GDP in 1900, at 18.6 per cent. By 1945, the proportion had dropped to 4.9 per cent. Pre-First World War levels were finally reached by 1980, at 17.7 per cent. But then came a massive acceleration, with the proportion hitting 56.8 per cent in 1995. In cultural terms, also, globalization is more powerful than ever before. Clearly, before 1914, educated people in Europe and the US had a common culture based on the classics, orchestral music, opera and so on. But the cinema, television and popular music mean that people from almost every country in the world will be able to recognize Arnold Schwarzenegger, Michael Jackson or Madonna. This is one factor that can cause great resentment, with some people feeling their culture is being swamped by American imports.

THE UK'S ROLE IN THE FINANCIAL SYSTEM

What is the effect of globalization in the UK? The UK economy may have had its problems but the UK's financial system has traditionally punched above its weight in global terms. The leading operators may well be US or European but they still choose London as their base. Even though the UK is not part of the eurozone, European banks have not left en masse for Frankfurt, the financial centre of the eurozone and home of the European Central Bank.

Some of this success as a financial centre is due to luck: the UK speaks the same language as the US, the world's leading economy and financial powerhouse. US bankers feel more comfortable in an English-speaking country; in addition, London seems a more attractive place to live than Frankfurt.

Some of the success is due to the UK regulatory regime, which has consistently been fairly welcoming to financial institutions. The financial reforms of the Conservative administration of 1979–97, and the higher-rate tax cuts it introduced, have played their part. The Labour government, which has been in office since 1997, has done little to reverse the trend.

It is now generally accepted that the UK needs to offer an economy that is appealing to foreign investors and foreign companies. The UK has been quite successful in attracting what is known as 'direct investment' from overseas companies: the building of factories, often in areas of high unemployment in Wales, Scotland or the North East. Politicians have argued that the UK has been successful in this quest because the government has cut taxes of corporate profits and because of more flexible labour markets (a euphemism for saying that companies face fewer problems in firing workers). Wider share ownership has also served the UK government's purpose. The cost of providing state pensions is a great burden on European countries, with their ageing populations. The Conservative government of 1979–97 cut this cost substantially, by linking future pension payments to prices rather than earnings. But the effect after twenty years is that the state pension now provides a pretty measly income.

UK citizens have therefore come to realize that they will depend on their own savings for a decent retirement income. Since shares have historically provided better returns than other assets, investors have welcomed government schemes such as personal equity plans and individual savings accounts which give tax breaks to savers. They have also opted for personal pension schemes, which offer tax advantages for long-term savers.

All this has fuelled the growth of the institutional investors mentioned in the Introduction and has meant that the majority of Britons have some kind of interest in the stock market.

But we have got ahead of ourselves. Before we discuss these issues in more detail, it is time to go back to first principles.

Figures taken from *Globalization and Growth in the Twentieth Century*, an IMF working paper by Nicholas Crafts.

2   **Money and Interest Rates**

MONEY

Primitive societies did not have money, since they did not trade. When trade began it was under a barter system. Goats might be exchanged for corn, or sheep for axes. As society became more complex, barter grew inadequate as a trading system. Goats might be acceptable as payment to one man but not to another, who might prefer sheep or cattle. Even then it was easy to dispute the question of how many sheep were worth a sack of corn.

Gradually precious metals and, most notably, gold and silver were used as payment and became the first money. Precious metals had several advantages. Money had to be scarce. It was no good basing a monetary system on the leaf. Everyone would soon grab all the leaves around and the smallest payment would require a wheelbarrowful. Money had also to be easy to carry and in divisible units – making the goat a poor monetary unit. Gold and silver were sufficiently scarce and sufficiently portable to meet society's requirements.

Of course, it soon became inconvenient to carry gold and silver ingots. Coins were created by the kings of Lydia in the eighth century BC.* From the days of Alexander the Great the custom began of depicting the head of the sovereign on coins.

There are a variety of functions which money serves. It is a *measure of value*. Sheep can be compared with goats and chalk with cheese by

---

* J. K. Galbraith, *Money: Whence it Came, Where it Went* (Penguin, 1976).

referring to the amount of money one would pay for each product. Money is also a *store of value*. It can be saved until it is needed, unlike the goods it buys, which are often perishable. Creditors will accept money as a future payment, confident that its value will remain stable in the meantime.

Of course, today's money is made from neither gold nor silver. Coins are made from copper or nickel, and the most valuable monetary units are made of paper. There are two main reasons for this. The first is that supplies of gold and silver were outstripped by the demands of society. If money is scarce, it is difficult for the economy to expand and for us to get richer. The second reason is the so-called Gresham's Law that 'bad money drives out good'. When money was in the form of gold coins, it was tempting for those with a large number of coins to shave off a tiny fraction of each coin. The resulting shavings could be melted down to make new coins. Gradually some coins contained less gold than others. Anyone who had a coin with the maximum amount of gold would have been foolish to spend it lest he received a coin with less gold in return. So the best coins were hoarded and the worst coins circulated. Bad money drove out good.

The earliest issues of money that was not backed by gold were known as *fiduciary* issues. Money is now totally divorced from its precious metal origins and seems unlikely to regress.

BANKNOTES AND CHEQUES

The next stages of the development of money – banknotes and cheques – are dealt with in Chapter 3, on the banks. It is sufficient to point out here that banknotes were, in origin, claims on gold and silver. Now money depends on the confidence of its users in the strength of the economy. When economies break down (as they occasionally do in wartime) money disappears and is replaced by some other commodity such as cigarettes.

As money has grown more sophisticated, so it has grown farther away from its origins. Banknotes replaced coins. Cheques replaced banknotes. Now debit and credit cards are steadily taking the place of cheques, and there are already moves towards 'electronic money', in the form of a card which you will charge up with cash and then use for shopping.

The system depends on the confidence of all those concerned. Shop-keepers accept cheques because banks will honour them. Bank accounts are therefore money in the same sense as notes and coins are, since they can be used instantly to purchase goods.

Banks can thus create money. This is because only a small proportion of the deposits they hold is needed to meet the claims of those who want to withdraw cash. Much of the need is met by those who deposit cash. A simple way for a bank to lend money is to create a deposit (or account) in someone's favour.

Suppose that a country has only one bank, which finds that it needs to keep 20 per cent of its deposits in the form of cash. It receives an extra £200 worth of cash deposits. The bank then buys £160 of British Telecom shares, leaving £40 cash free to meet any claims from depositors. The person from whom it bought the shares now has £160 in cash, which is deposited with the bank. So the bank has £360 in deposits (the original £200 plus the new deposit of £160), of which it needs to keep only £72 (20 per cent) in the form of cash. The bank is therefore able to increase its total investments to £288 (£360 − £72) and can buy a further £128 of BT shares. Once again the person from whom it buys the shares will receive cash, depositing this with the bank. This process will continue until the bank has deposits of £1,000, of which £200 is held in the form of cash. The bank's balance sheet will then look like this:

ASSETS		LIABILITIES	
Cash	£200	Customer deposits	£1,000
BT shares	£800		
TOTAL	£1,000		£1,000

(Note that customer deposits are a liability, since they might at any time have to be repaid.)

To find out the total amounts of deposits that can be created from the original cash base, divide 100 by the percentage which the bank needs to hold as cash (known as the *cash ratio*). Then multiply the result by the amount of the original deposit. Thus, in this example, dividing 100 by the cash ratio of 20 per cent gives 5, and multiplying that by the original deposit equals £1,000.

The cash ratio is therefore very important. If, in the example, the ratio had been only 10 per cent, the amount of deposits created from the original deposit would have been £2,000 and not £1,000. In practice, banks find that they need to keep around 8 per cent of their deposits in the form of cash.

This relation between the money which banks need to hold in liquid form and the amount which they can lend has, in the past, been used by the Bank of England to control the level of credit in the economy (see Chapter 4).

DEFINING THE MONEY SUPPLY

As money has become increasingly sophisticated, so it has become more and more difficult to define exactly what it is. This issue assumed particular importance with the prominence of the monetarist school of economics, which believed that the level of inflation is closely related to the rate of increase of the money supply. In the late 1970s and early 1980s many Western governments, including the UK's, were strong adherents of the monetarist school and attempted to base economic policies on its theories. Accordingly, they needed to define the money supply before they could control it.

The Bank of England publishes several definitions of money. M1 is defined as notes and coins in circulation with the public, plus sterling current accounts held by the private sector. M2 is M1 plus private-sector sterling deposit accounts held with the deposit (commercial) banks and discount houses (see Chapters 3 and 5). A broader definition, M3, includes virtually all the deposits held by the private and public sectors in both sterling and foreign currencies. Sterling M3, which was for many years the government's principal monetary target, is M3 minus the foreign currency element. As something of an afterthought, the Bank devised a very narrow definition of money, M0, which consists purely of notes and coins.

By defining money solely by reference to deposits held in banks, the Bank of England realized that it was failing to take into account other deposits which might be substitutes for those in banks. For example, building society deposits are not strictly compatible with bank deposits. Traditionally it was not possible to write a cheque on a building society account, although this too has changed. However, if building society rates are more attractive than those offered by the banks, depositors will switch their money from their bank accounts to a building society. Most society accounts will let their depositors withdraw cash instantly, and many creditors will accept a building society cheque as payment. To call bank deposits money and building society accounts non-money would be to paint an inaccurate picture of credit levels in the economy.

The Bank of England accordingly established a new set of definitions of money, the Private Sector Liquidity (PSL series). PSL1 includes notes and coins, sterling bank deposits, certificates of deposits, Treasury and bank bills and similar instruments. PSL2 adds in building society deposits and shares and deposits with similar institutions. Eventually, a broad definition along these lines was named M4. However, the PSL definitions have attracted little attention from economic analysts.

In the middle of 1985 the Chancellor of the Exchequer effectively abandoned sterling M3 as a target figure for his monetary policy. It had been growing at 20 per cent a year at a time when inflation was falling. It was announced that Mo would continue to be watched (along with short-term interest rates and the exchange rate).

The authorities still publish figures for the levels of Mo and M4. But although the measures were still seen as useful indicators, it was generally agreed that monetary targets could not be used as mechanical devices for setting economic policy. The measures were simply too erratic, and prone to distortion by developments in the financial markets.

INTEREST RATES

Money on its own is a very useful but, in the long run, unprofitable possession. That £200 stashed under the mattress will in five years' time still be only £200. In the meantime inflation will have eroded its purchasing power, so that it may be able to purchase only half as many goods as it could five years before. Had the money been deposited with a building society, however, interest would have been added every six months. At 10 per cent a year the original cash deposit would have increased to £322.10 at the end of the five-year period. This interest rate is essentially the *price* of money. The price is paid by the borrower in return for the use of the lender's money. The lender is compensated for *not* having the use of his money.

There are two alternative methods of calculating interest: *simple* and *compound*.

Simple interest can be easily explained. If a deposit of £100 is placed in a building society and simple interest of 10 per cent per annum is paid, then after one year the deposit will be £110, after two years £120 and so on. Nearly all interest is paid, however, on a compound basis.

Compound interest involves the payment of interest on previous interest. In the above example the depositor would still receive £10 interest in the first year. In the second year, however, interest would be calculated on £110, rather than on £100. The depositor would thus earn £11 interest in the second year, bringing his deposit to £121. In the third year he would earn £12.10 interest and so on. The cumulative effect is impressive. The same £100 deposit would become £350 after twenty-five years of simple interest but £1,083.50 with compound interest. Most savings accounts operate on the principle of compound interest, but most securities pay only simple interest. A bond may pay 5 per cent a year but only on the principal amount borrowed. That amount does not increase over the bond's lifetime.

When dealing with a bond or with a share, it is more important to talk of the *yield* than merely of the interest rate or dividend.

YIELD

A deposit account in a building society carries an annual interest rate. The money deposited will always be returned in full with the accumulated interest, but the lump sum (capital) will not grow. Other investments, like shares, bonds and houses, are not as safe as a building society account but offer the potential for capital growth. Shares, bonds and property can all increase in price as well as provide income in the form of dividends, interest or rent. Since the price of these securities can alter, the interest rate or dividend will be more or less significant as the price falls or rises. The interest rate or dividend, expressed as a percentage of the price of the asset, is the *yield*. A security with a price of £80 that pays interest of £8 a year has a yield of 10 per cent. If the value of the security rises to £100, the yield will fall to 8 per cent. In assessing the profitability of various assets, calculating their yield is very important; articles in the financial press will talk about equity yields and bond yields as much as about dividends and interest rates.

Until the 1950s, the yield on shares was higher than that on most bonds, since shares were perceived as a riskier form of investment. Since then, shares have offered lower yields than bonds or savings accounts because the prospects of capital growth are much greater.

Probably the best way of showing the importance of yields is to cite the bond market. Suppose that in a year of low interest rates the Jupiter Corporation issues a bond with a face value of £100 and an interest rate (normally called the coupon) of 5 per cent. In the following year interest rates rise and bond investors demand a return of 10 per cent from newly issued bonds. Those investors who bought Jupiter bonds are now stuck with bonds which give them only half the market rate. Many of them will therefore sell their Jupiter bonds and buy newly issued bonds.

Who will they sell the bonds to? Potential buyers of Jupiter bonds will be no more willing to accept a yield of only 5 per cent than the sellers. Bond sellers will therefore have to accept a reduced price for the Jupiter bonds. The price will have to fall until the returns from Jupiter and other bonds are roughly equal. If the bond price fell from £100 to £50, then each year bondholders would still receive £5 on a bond which cost them £50 – a return, or yield, of 10 per cent. The Jupiter bond would be as attractive as a bond priced at £100 with a 10 per cent coupon, which would also yield 10 per cent.

Calculating the yield on a bond is not quite that easy, however. The bond will be repaid at some future point. Say, for example, it has a nominal value of £100, sells for £96, pays £5 interest a year and has one year to go before it is repaid. Over the next year the bondholder will receive £5 interest and £4 capital – the difference between the £96 it sells for and the £100 which will be repaid. So the bond yields £9 on a price of £96, just under 10 per cent. A yield which is calculated to allow for capital repayment is called the *gross yield to redemption*. Going back to the Jupiter issue, the bonds would not have to fall in price as low as £50 to keep their yields in line. If they had a five-year maturity, they would have to fall only to around £83 to have a gross yield to redemption of about 10 per cent. Bond trading depends on quick and sophisticated calculation of yields and exploitation of anomalies in the market.

This process of adjusting prices to bring yields in line gives bond investors the prospect of capital gain (or loss) on their holdings. An investor who buys Jupiter bonds at £100 would lose £25 if the price fell to £75 because of the yield adjustment. That would more than wipe out any interest earned on the bond. However, if the interest rate offered on other bonds fell back to 5 per cent again, then Jupiter's bonds would climb back to their face value of £100. An investor who bought at the low of £75 would have made a capital gain of 33 per cent and still earned interest in the process.

Because of the yield factor, bond prices have an inverse relationship with interest rates: bond markets are generally euphoric when interest rates are falling, depressed when they are rising.

INTEREST-RATE DETERMINANTS

Having understood the difference between simple and compound interest and the importance of yields, we can now look at the factors that determine an interest rate. In fact, it is more correct to talk of interest *rates*. At any one time a host of different rates are charged throughout the economy. So it is important to distinguish the determinants of specific interest rates as well as those which affect the general level of rates in the economy.

First, let us look at the determinants of specific rates. One of the principal elements is risk. There is always the chance, whomever money is lent to, that it will not be repaid. That risk will be reflected in a higher interest rate. This is one of the general principles of finance. The riskier the investment, the higher the return demanded by the investor. It is a principle which sometimes is ignored, mainly because investors do not always assess risk adequately. Nevertheless, it is a useful principle to bear in mind, especially when it is stood on its head. Those investors who seek extremely high returns would be wise to remember that such investments normally involve extremely high risk.

Governments are usually presumed to be the least risky debtors of all, at least by lenders in their own country. (Other countries' governments are a different matter, as many banks who lent to Brazil and Argentina have discovered.) But the government of a lender's country can always print more money to repay the debt if necessary. In any case, if the government does not repay debt, it is reasonable for investors to presume that no one else in the country will.

Banks have traditionally been rated next on the credit ladder. Nowadays, however, many large corporations are considered better credit risks than even the biggest banks. For the benefit of potential investors, some agencies have devised elaborate rating systems to assess the creditworthiness of banks and corporations (see Chapter 10).

At the bottom of the ratings come individuals like you and me. Individuals have a sad tendency to lose jobs, get sick, over-commit themselves and default on their loans. Unless they are exceptionally wealthy, individuals thus pay the highest interest rates of all.

One of the other main elements involved is liquidity. The house buyer with a mortgage has to pay a higher rate than is received by the building society depositor because the society needs to be compensated for the loss of liquidity involved in tying up its money for twenty-five years. The society faces the risk that it will at some point need the funds that it has lent to the house buyer but will be unable to gain access to them. As I mentioned in the introduction, this is another of the basic principles of finance. The more liquid the asset, the lower the return. The most liquid asset of all, cash, bears no interest at all.

Logical though the above arguments are, it often happens that long-term interest rates are below short-term rates. To understand why, we must look at the yield curve.

THE YIELD CURVE

We have already proposed a general principle of finance – that lesser liquidity demands greater reward. That being the case, longer-term instruments should always bear a higher interest rate than short-term ones. This is not always true. Long-term rates can be the same as, or lower than, those of short-term instruments.

A curve can be drawn which links the different levels of rates with the different maturities of debt. If long-term rates are above short-term ones, this is described as a *positive* or upward-sloping yield curve. If short-term rates are higher, the curve is described as *negative* or *inverted*.

What determines the shape of the yield curve? The three main theories used to explain its structure are the liquidity theory, the expectations theory and the market-segmentation theory.

The *liquidity theory*, which has already been outlined, states simply that investors will demand an extra reward (in the form of a higher interest rate) for investing their money for a long period. They may do so because they fear that they will need the funds suddenly but will be unable to obtain them, or they may be worried about the possibility of default. Borrowers (in particular, businesses) will be prepared to pay higher interest rates in order to secure long-term funds for investment. Thus, other things being equal, the yield curve will be upward-sloping.

The *expectations* theory holds that the yield curve represents investors' views on the likely future movement of short-term interest rates. If one-year interest rates are 10 per cent and an investor expects them to rise to 12 per cent in a year's time, he will be unwilling to accept 10 per cent on a two-year loan. It would be more profitable for him to lend for one year and then re-lend his money at the higher rate. A two-year loan will therefore have to offer at least 11 per cent a year before the investor will be attracted. Thus if interest rates are expected to *rise*, the yield curve will be *upward-sloping*. If investors expect short-term interest rates to *fall*, however, they will seek to lend long-term. That will increase the supply of long-term funds and bring down their price (i.e. long-term interest rates). Thus the yield curve will be *downward-sloping*.

What determines investors' expectations of future interest-rate movements? Much may depend on future inflation rates. If inflation is set to rise, then price rises will absorb much of an investor's interest income. So investors will demand higher rates when they think inflation is set to increase.

The economist John Maynard Keynes constructed a more elaborate theory which depended on the yield of securities. If people expect interest rates to rise, Keynes argued, they will hold on to their money in the form of cash, in order to avoid capital loss. But if they expect rates to fall, they will invest their money to profit from capital gains. Of course, this principle applies to bonds rather than to interest-bearing accounts. As we have seen, if interest rates rise, the price of previously issued bonds falls until investors earn a similar yield from equivalent bonds. Thus a bond investor who expected rates to rise will sell his bonds before the rise in rates and the resultant fall in the bond price occurs. The investor will hold the funds in the most liquid form available so that he can reinvest them as soon as rates rise. If the same investor expects interest rates to fall, he will hold on to the bonds because their price will rise as rates fall.

The third theory of the yield curve is the *market-segmentation* theory. This assumes that the markets for the different maturities of debt instruments are entirely separate. Within each segment interest rates are set by supply and demand. The shape of the yield curve will be determined by the different results of supply/demand trade-offs. If a lot of borrowers have long-term financing needs and few investors want to lend for such periods, the curve will be upward-sloping. If borrowers demand short-term funds and investors prefer to lend for longer periods, the curve will be downward-sloping.

ECONOMIC THEORIES ON THE GENERAL LEVEL OF INTEREST RATES

We have already looked at the factors which affect the level of interest rates for different maturities, instruments and borrowers. It is also worth considering theories which concern the general level of rates in the economy.

As already mentioned, the rate of inflation is generally accepted to be a substantial ingredient of interest rates. Lenders normally expect interest rates at least to compensate them for the effect of rising prices. They therefore watch closely the *real* interest rate – that is, the interest received after inflation has been taken into account. Historically, real interest rates have averaged around 2–3 per cent; that is, if inflation were 7 per cent, interest rates would be 9–10 per cent. However, this relationship is far from permanent: real interest rates have been, at times, negative (below the rate of inflation), and at times in the 1980s they were as high as 8 per cent, making that a very good time to lend.

The most important inflation rate is the rate which a lender *expects* to occur during the lifetime of his or her investment. The inflation rate which is published by the government, the consumer price index, gives only the *previous year*'s price rises, but it is *next year*'s price rises which will affect the value of the lender's investment. So lenders must undertake a difficult piece of economic forecasting.

It is very important to remember that financial markets are now international. Rates in Britain cannot be separated from those in other countries. UK investors can invest abroad if there is the chance for higher rates overseas, and foreign investors can invest here if UK rates are above their own. Both decisions are linked with the level of exchange rates. An investment in the USA might yield a high dollar rate of return, but if the dollar fell against sterling, investors would find themselves worse off.

Governments concerned about the level of interest rates will often intervene to try to influence their movement. They may be concerned about the exchange rate and may push interest rates up to defend the pound. Alternatively, they may be concerned about the amount of credit in the economy. People may be borrowing because interest rates are low, with the result that excessive demand is leading to inflationary pressures.

The classical explanation of the level of interest rates is associated with the theory of supply and demand. Thus the interest rate is the balancing point between the flow of funds from savers and the need for investment funds from business. If more funds become available from savers, or if industry has less need to borrow, interest rates will fall. If the funds available from savers are reduced, or if industry has a greater need to borrow, interest rates will rise. The demand for funds is likely to be affected by business people's expectations of future profits. If they believe that they will achieve a high rate of return on investment, they will be willing to borrow.

The supply of funds for borrowers depends largely on the willingness of the personal sector to save. Why do people save? One of the main reasons is to provide for old age or for children and spouses in the event of early death. This form of saving normally takes the form of investment in pension funds and life assurance and is helped by tax advantages. There has been a substantial growth in this form of saving since the 1960s. Another reason is to guard against rainy days caused by illness or unemployment: by its nature, such saving needs to be very liquid and is normally placed in building societies or interest-bearing bank accounts. A third reason for saving is to allow for major purchases or for holidays: again, such savings need a liquid home like a building society account.

Just as important as the reasons why people save are the reasons why the proportion of their income that they save changes over time. A certain amount of wealth is necessary before people can save – if all someone's income is needed just to pay for food and rent, there will be no money left to save. However, it is not correct to assume the reverse: that the larger a person's income, the more he or she saves. The highest income-earners are often among the biggest *borrowers*, since banks will extend credit only to those who they think will be able to repay. The greater a person's income, therefore, the greater the possibility for incurring debt. Debt is negative saving. In fact, the cautious middle classes have traditionally been the biggest savers.

However, academic explanations of movements in the savings ratio (the proportion of income which is saved) have focused on income levels. If income rises, according to theory, there will be a larger increase in the level of savings; if income falls, savings will drop disproportionately as people run down their incomes to pay for their expenditure.

During the inflationary 1970s the savings ratio increased sharply, much to most economists' surprise. Since inflation erodes the purchasing power of savings, it was assumed that consumers would run down their cash balances and deposits, which bear a negative real interest rate, and would prefer to hold physical assets such as property, the value of which tends to increase in line with inflation.

What seems to have happened instead is that savers, perhaps for the rainy-day reasons outlined above, were concerned to maintain the purchasing power of their savings. Because of the rate of inflation, they needed to save a greater proportion of their income merely to keep the value of their savings constant. The rise in the savings ratio in the 1970s was followed by an equally sharp decline in the 1980s as inflation fell and it became easier to maintain the value of savings.

Saving seems to have a clear correlation to the state of the economy. In times of boom, people tend to save less. They are more confident about their job prospects and are happy to borrow money to make expensive purchases, such as cars and durable goods. In times of economic slowdown, they cut back their expenditure because they are less confident about their job prospects.

In analysing savings patterns an important distinction to recognize is that between committed and discretionary savings. Committed savings are made up of contributions to life assurance and pensions schemes and, as such, are relatively inflexible to changes in income. Discretionary savings represent payments into building society accounts or perhaps unit trusts. Such savings adjust much more quickly to income movements. Repayment of a mortgage represents committed savings in that it is an investment in the value of a real asset (i.e. a house).

Indeed, many believe that the housing market has distorted UK savings patterns. Years of inflation, and the favourable tax treatment of home ownership, has taught British investors that property is the safest store of wealth.

What does seem clear is that the greater sophistication of the modern financial system causes interest rates to move more frequently than ever before.

3

The Banks

Banks are at the heart of the financial system. They are the one type of financial institution with which all of us are bound to come into contact at some point in our lives. To appreciate their importance, we must first look at their origins.

THE FIRST BANKERS

Gold and silver have traditionally been the two predominant monetary metals for the reasons outlined in Chapter 2. As a result, goldsmiths and silversmiths became the earliest bankers. Nervous citizens, who were well aware of the dangers of keeping their gold under the mattress, began to use the smiths, who had safes to store their wares, as a place to keep their wealth. In return, the smiths would give the depositor a handwritten receipt. It soon became easier for the depositors to pay their creditors with the smiths' receipts, rather than go through the time-consuming process of recovering the gold or silver and giving it to the creditor, who might only re-deposit it with the smith. Creditors were willing to accept the receipts as payment, provided that they were sure that they could always redeem the receipts for gold or silver when necessary.

The receipts were the first banknotes. The legacy of those early receipts is visible today in the form of the confident statement on banknotes: 'I promise to pay the bearer on demand the sum of . . .'

Despite having the image of the Queen to back it up, that statement is of no value today and anyone attempting to redeem a five pound note for gold at his local bank will be disappointed.

Smart goldsmiths were able to take the development of banking one stage further. They noticed that of the gold stored in their safes, only a small quantity was ever required for withdrawal and that amount was roughly matched by fresh deposits. There was therefore a substantial quantity of money sitting idle. The money could be lent (and interest earned) in the knowledge that the day-to-day requirements of depositors could still easily be covered (see Chapter 2).

THE ITALIAN INFLUENCE

Among the earliest bankers were goldsmiths and silversmiths from the Lombardy region of Italy who were granted land in London by King Edward I. One of the sites they received – Lombard Street – is at the heart of the modern City of London. Back in Italy, the money lenders had conducted their business from wooden benches in market places. The Italian word for bench, *banco*, was corrupted by the English into 'bank'. The Italians were also responsible for introducing the symbols that were synonymous with British money until 1971 – £, s. and d., or *lire*, *soldi* and *denarii*. It is a nice irony that those who wear the £ symbol as a signal of opposition to Europe are in fact displaying an Italian figure.

Many of the early bankers misjudged their ability to absorb 'runs' – times of financial panic when investors rushed to claim back their gold. In such cases, bankers had insufficient funds to meet the claims of depositors upon them and thus became 'bankrupt' (literally 'broken bench'). Such runs could easily become self-fulfilling. As soon as depositors feared that a bank might become bankrupt, they would flock to the banks in order to demand their money back, thus accelerating the bank's deterioration into ruin. Because of the nature of banking, no bank could stand a determined run. Some tried ingenious methods to do so. One bank arranged for a few wealthy depositors to arrive by carriage at the front of the bank and withdraw their gold ostentatiously. The queuing small depositors were impressed. Meanwhile, the wealthy depositors sent their footmen round the back to re-deposit the gold, so it could be used to meet the claims of the other depositors.

Bankruptcies did not reduce the total number of banks. The seeming ease with which it was possible to make money from banking soon attracted others to take the places of the institutions that had failed. Gradually, depositors regained confidence in the trustworthiness of the banks. Thus began a regular banking cycle of boom and bust. Professor Galbraith explains that the length of these cycles 'came to accord roughly with the time it took people to forget the last disaster – for the financial geniuses of one generation to die in disrepute and be replaced by new craftsmen who the gullible and the gulled could believe had, this time but truly, the Midas touch'.*

In the UK Charles I, that unlikely saint, gave banking an unwitting boost in 1640 by seizing £130,000, which merchants had unwisely committed to his safe-keeping by placing it in the Royal Mint. Merchants decided that in future it would be rather safer to deposit their funds with the bankers in the City. It was not until 1694 that the government's financial reputation could be restored and the Bank of England established: by that time, the crown was on the head of the sober and respectable Dutchman, William of Orange.

MODERN BANKING

The history of the Bank of England is considered in Chapter 4. This section considers the modern banks which have grown out of the early activities of the goldsmiths.

There are many varieties of banks, but the two types that are best known in Britain are the retail and the merchant, or investment, banks. Investment banks are considered later in the chapter and are best known for arranging complex financial deals and for financing trade. Retail banks take deposits from customers and lend them out to companies and insolvent individuals.

The banks which most people know, and are indeed at the heart of the UK financial system, are the clearing banks, so called because individual transactions between them are cleared through the London Clearing House system. This saves the banks, and therefore their customers, a lot of time. Rather than have Lloyds pay over £20 to Barclays for Mr Brown's

* J. K. Galbraith, *Money: Whence it Came, Where it Went* (Penguin, 1976).

gas bill and Barclays pay £15 to HSBC for Mrs Smith's shopping, the clearing house tots up all the individual transactions and arrives with a net position for each bank at the end of the day. Lloyds might owe NatWest £20,000 and HSBC owe Barclays £15,000 – the important fact is that on a daily basis, each bank is involved in only one clearing house transaction with any other.

CHAPS

In 1984, the clearing process was much improved by the introduction of the Clearing House Automated Payment System (CHAPS), which replaced the old manual system for processing cheques and bankers' payments. Rather than laboriously adding up the total of each bank's payments and receipts by hand, a CHAPS payment results in an adjustment to a running total held on the system. At the end of the day, each bank has logged up a deficit or surplus vis-à-vis the other banks in the system. Payments are cleared in a few minutes rather than the hour and a half of the old system.

The work that the clearing banks handle is huge. In mid 1998, CHAPS was handling an average of 70,000 payments worth £150bn each day.

The big challenge for payment systems has come with the advent of the European single currency, the euro, which the UK has not joined in the first wave. The European Monetary Institute has set up the Target system for making payments between the clearing banks of the Euro member countries. But CHAPS has responded by making sure it can settle Euro payments from the outset, which should allow British banks to stay competitive.

Many building societies have converted into banks in recent years but the 'big four' – Lloyds, National Westminster (now part of Royal Bank of Scotland), HSBC and Barclays are still the best known banks in England, with over 10,000 branches between them. Although the services they provide are virtually identical, each has its own personality and problems.

Barclays Bank was originally an amalgamation of Quaker family banks. Although it can claim credit for being the first to introduce such ideas as the credit card and the automated teller machine, it was dogged for years by its reputation for being heavily involved in South African investment.

Periodically, Barclays' annual meetings were disrupted by dissident share-holders and its branches picketed by protesters.

Barclays invested heavily in the field of investment banking, building up an operation called Barclays de Zoete Wedd or BZW. But in 1997, the group's chief executive, Martin Taylor, decided to sell off the equities part of the BZW business, on the grounds that it earned insufficient returns.

The bank still has an investment banking arm, Barclays Capital, which focuses on the bond markets but it has given up its ambitions of being a global investment bank on the lines of Merrill Lynch. Even this more limited arm ran up heavy losses in the Russian financial crisis of 1998. Following these developments, Martin Taylor resigned in November 1998.

It has a strong presence in fund management, where Barclays Global Investors is the second biggest management group in the world, with a particular expertise in tracking stock market indices.

Lloyds has avoided some of the mistakes of its rivals by concentrating on retail financial services. It pulled out of investment banking in the 1980s and then built up its retail presence by acquiring the building society, Cheltenham & Gloucester, and the bank, TSB; since the latter purchase, it has become known as Lloyds TSB.

After a long struggle to resolve its problems on its own, Midland Bank agreed to a takeover by the Hong Kong and Shanghai Banking Corporation in 1992 (despite a rival bid from Lloyds). Midland never really recovered from the blows it suffered when it acquired the California-based Crocker Bank, and even the best efforts of Sir Kit McMahon, former Deputy Governor of the Bank of England, failed to restore it to health. HSBC is a huge global bank in its own right, with an investment bank-ing operation, HSBC Securities, formed from Midland Montagu (the Midland securities arm) and the broker James Capel. In late 1998, HSBC announced that the Midland name would disappear from the high street by the end of the decade.

National Westminster Bank was formed when the National Provincial and Westminster Banks merged in 1968. It survived a crisis of confidence in 1974, when it made the unwise step of issuing a statement assuring investors that it was not in trouble (a sure way of making people believe the opposite).

Like the other banks, NatWest has gone through a lot of change in recent years. It has moved out of its 600 foot high tower and it has retreated from a foray into investment banking (which caused a lot of embarrassment when the subsidiary, County NatWest, was tied up in the Blue Arrow affair). A large part of the operation was eventually sold off to the US investment bank, Bankers Trust.

In late 1999 and early 2000, NatWest faced rival bids from two Scottish banks, Bank of Scotland and Royal Bank of Scotland. The latter's offer proved successful although the Bank of Scotland then went on to merge with the former building society, the Halifax.

The disposal of the bulk of Barclays and NatWest's securities operations, and the purchase of Midland by HSBC, means that there is now no British bank which is trying to compete with the world's largest by offering a comprehensive service with everything from deposits to share trading.

The problem with such a concept is that it is highly expensive and very risky – the top traders need high salaries and a lot of capital to play with. The British banks seem largely to have settled for the safer, but less glamorous, area of domestic personal and corporate banking.

THE IMPORTANCE OF RETAIL DEPOSITS

The big four banks have long had a built-in advantage over their rivals – the current accounts of ordinary depositors like you and me. Such accounts traditionally paid no interest whereas the banks could charge as much as 20 per cent on overdrafts – a fairly hefty profit margin. Banks without retail deposits have to borrow at market rates in the money market in order to obtain funds. It can be said in justification of the retail banks that the costs of such a large network of branches, in terms of buildings, staff and paperwork, take a substantial slice of that margin.

This so-called endowment effect started to disappear in the 1980s when competition from building societies forced the banks to offer interest-bearing accounts. But the decline in interest rates in the early 1990s meant that interest rates started to fall to very low levels. Indeed, the banks began to contemplate charging for the services, such as clearing cheques, which they had previously provided free to customers.

By the end of the 1990s, these retail deposits were looking as much of a burden as a boon. The problem was that servicing those depositors required the maintenance of a vast and expensive branch network.

Rivals emerged with the ability to 'cherry pick' the best retail customers. One group was the supermarkets, which offered interest-bearing accounts to their customers. Another was Internet banks, which were able to offer interest-bearing accounts without the need for branch networks. The big banks reacted by cutting costs, laying off staff and closing banks in rural areas and small towns. They also encouraged investors to switch to banking over the telephone or the Internet, and focused on other higher-margin products such as life insurance and fund management. The most sought-after banking customer in the late 1990s was the so-called HNWI – high net worth individual.

THE CREDIT CARD

One innovation has changed the banking market more than anything else in recent years – the credit card. In the UK, Barclays was the first on the market with the Barclaycard and the other banks responded with Access. Now most cards are part of two international systems, Visa and MasterCard (which has replaced the Access name in the UK).

But consumers no longer have to choose between the cards offered by the high street banks. With US operators such as MBNA moving into the market, the choice has vastly increased. By the end of 1997, the UK consumer could select from 1,200 cards, issued by around 20 main issuers, in a market worth £60bn a year.

The market has gone through several phases as consumers sought the best deal and card issuers sought to find ways to make money. Card issuers make their money both from the interest charged to users and from fees paid by retailers when the goods are bought.

Smart consumers realized early on that, rather than pay the high (over 20 per cent) interest charges imposed by the issuers, it was best to pay off the bill in full each month. Issuers responded by imposing annual fees, payable regardless of your credit status. But then competition in the market meant that some issuers started to attract users by offering no fee deals – and fees started to be phased out.

In the retailing market, some stores reacted to the issuers' fees either by refusing to accept credit cards, or by adopting their own cards (Marks & Spencer was an obvious example). The widespread popularity of cards, however, and the long-running £50 limit on cheque payments, meant many stores had to give ground, with even Marks & Spencer forced to accept other people's cards.

Recent developments in the market have included affinity cards, which link the holder to some organization (a charity, old college or football club), often with some small payment going to the organization every time the card is used; the use of special introductory low interest rates, encouraging users to switch their debt from one card to another; and the use of bonus points for frequent use (one example is the Goldfish card, linked to British Gas).

But there are many other card variants in the market. Indeed electronic money is fast becoming the dominant means of exchange.

- Charge cards. These are cards (the obvious example is American Express) which do not allow you credit but require you to pay off the balance at the end of the month. Instead of interest therefore, you pay a fee.
- Debit cards. These cards (the common ones in the UK are Switch and Delta) take money straight out of your current account so do not give the consumer any credit at all. They offer an obvious alternative to cash.
- Cashpoint cards. Cards that simply allow the user to remove money from an ATM (automated teller machine) or hole-in-the-wall. These cards are now often combined with debit cards.
- Loyalty cards. Not the same as store cards but issued by retailers. Frequent use earns the consumer 'points' which can be redeemed for cash or discounts on other goods. Around 40m cards have now been issued.
- E-cards or electronic cards. These could be the wave of the future although, as yet, they are proving slow to catch on. Rather than carry cash, the user simply charges up the card with money. The retailer electronically scans the card to receive payment. The idea is to use the card for small transactions where credit or debit cards are too cumbersome.

For banks, credit cards are a reasonably profitable business because of the high interest rates paid by those who fail to pay off their balances each month. But they face two problems; bad debts and fraud.

A rise in bad debts has been an inevitable consequence of the more widespread use of credit cards; many people get regular solicitations to take up cards through the mail and those who have cards often find that the issuer regularly increases their credit limit.

The battle against fraud is fought on two fronts; preventing people from printing fake cards (often by the use of holograms); and preventing the use of stolen cards. There has been talk for years of using photographs on cards but as yet the practice has not caught on.

ASSETS AND LIABILITIES

Banks' assets are the loans and investments which they make with the deposits provided and which earn them interest. Those assets are held in a variety of forms. A substantial proportion is lent out short-term – either at call (effectively overnight) or in the form of short-term deposits in the money markets (see Chapter 5). The bulk of banks' assets is held in the form of loans – to individuals and to businesses. Individuals borrow mainly in the form of overdrafts which have advantages for the banks since they can, in theory, recall them overnight. That gives the flexibility in case of a sudden drop in their funds.

The banks also lend longer-term, both domestically and internationally. In the UK, the loans are vital to the development of industry. Most companies start with the help of a bank loan, usually secured on the assets of a company. That means that if the firm folds, the bank has a claim on the firm's fixed capital such as machinery or buildings.

The proportion of the banks' assets which they need to hold in the form of cash is known as the cash ratio. The ratio has from time to time been set by the Bank of England to ensure that banks remain sound. It determines to some extent the total amount banks can lend. However, there are other factors involved.

One of the most important is the supply of creditworthy customers. Banks are normally cautious about the people to whom they grant overdrafts. If we assume that the number of people who are good credit risks (i.e. they have a steady job, good references, a good financial record) remains fairly constant, that puts a limit on banks' expansion.

The general state of the economy will also affect the growth of bank lending. If the economy is healthy, more businesses will be seeking to borrow funds to finance their investment plans. If the economy is in recession, however, few industries will be prepared to invest and therefore to borrow. Banks might seek to attract more borrowers by lowering their interest rates, but there is an obvious limit to such a process. The banks cannot afford the return from their lending to fall below the cost of their borrowing. The return from lending must always be significantly higher, because of the substantial costs involved in running a branch network.

Banks tend to follow a feast-and-famine process. Lots of loans will be made in times of economic boom, but when the economy starts to contract, some of those loans will fail to be repaid. That will prompt banks to suffer losses in the form of write-downs of their loan portfolios. If the bad debts are substantial, as occurred in Japan during the 1990s, the future of individual banks may be threatened.

FORMER BUILDING SOCIETIES

A number of building societies (see Chapter 6) have converted to banking status in recent years. The first to do so was Abbey National, but some of the biggest societies eventually followed suit including the Halifax, Woolwich and Alliance & Leicester.

Traditional building societies are mutual organizations, that is they are owned by their savers and borrowers rather than shareholders. That has some advantages to the savers and borrowers. Instead of paying out profits to shareholders, the profits can be used to increase (or for borrowers, reduce) the societies' interest rates.

However, societies have still converted for two reasons. First, the management of the societies themselves have wanted to expand into new areas, such as life insurance or corporate lending. That is difficult to do within the fairly cumbersome structure of a building society.

Secondly, conversion involves the issue of apparently free shares to the society's members, which they regard as pure profit. Traditionalists argue that members will suffer in the end because they will receive lower rates (as savers) or pay higher rates (as borrowers) but most people seem ready to take the money and run.

POST OFFICE

It occurred to nineteenth-century governments that small savers (some of whom were depositors at the Trustee Savings Banks) were a very useful source of funds for the National Debt (the gap between the government's revenue and expenditure). At the time, the nation's private banks served only a very select band of customers. The government accordingly opened up the Post Office Savings Bank to tap these funds. It soon became the nation's largest repository for savings, thanks to the advantage of a large number of branches. Not always the most competitive of banks, it paid a standard interest rate of 2.5 per cent from around 1900 until 1970.

Following a change of name to the National Savings Bank, the government had offered a wide variety of savings schemes from Index-linked SAYE (Save As You Earn) to Granny bonds. Although these were rather more competitive than the Post Office used to be, the government's healthy finances (and a general fall in private saving) kept National Savings out of the limelight.

In Post Offices, customers can also get access to many banking services through the Girobank, which is now owned by the Alliance & Leicester.

MERCHANT AND INVESTMENT BANKS

The high street banks are household names. But while merchant and investment banks such as Merrill Lynch are very well known in the US, their UK equivalents never became household names and most have now been taken over by US and European groups. Mainly, this is because they have few direct dealings with the public and have no high street outlets.

It is very difficult to define exactly what a merchant bank is: one of the main guides to the business says that merchant bankers are now 'seldom merchants and by no means always bankers'.* The other name by which merchant banks used to be known is that of *accepting houses*, referring to their habit of accepting bills of exchange as a means of financing com-

---

* C. J. J. Clay and B. S. Wheble, *Modern Merchant Banking*, 2nd edn, rev. L. H. L. Cohen (Woodhead-Faulkner, 1983).

panies' trading activities. That term now refers to only a tiny fraction of their activities.

THE GROWTH OF MERCHANT BANKING

Before the development of a worldwide banking system, much international trade depended on trust – trust that goods would be delivered and that they would be paid for. It was much easier for overseas clients to trust merchants with whom they had traded before or those with whom their friends had traded. Thus, the larger and well-established merchants found it easier to trade than their smaller and less familiar competitors.

The smaller firms needed some way both of assuring their clients that they were trustworthy, and of raising money to cover the interval between the time goods were delivered and the time they were paid for. The normal method for raising finance in this period was for the exporter to draw up a bill of exchange, whose value was a large proportion of the value of the goods being sold. The exporter could then sell the bill to a local banker at a discount and receive a substantial proportion of the money in advance. The extent of the bank's discount would represent two elements, a charge equivalent to interest on what was effectively a loan and a charge reflecting the risk of non-payment.

Small exporters found the banks would often charge a very large discount to advance money on their bills, if they agreed to do so at all. So the smaller merchants began to ask their larger brethren to guarantee (or accept) their bills. In the event that the small merchant failed to pay up, the large merchant would be liable. In return for the service, the large merchants charged an acceptance commission, based on a percentage of the size of the bill.

Eventually, some of these large merchants found that they could earn more money from their finance activities than from their trading and became full-time merchant banks or accepting houses. For a long time, their business was centred around the financing of trade but gradually, as they developed a reputation for financial acumen, they increased the corporate finance side of their activities.

Many merchant banks were begun by immigrants, refugees or Jews, shut out of the rather stuffy world of the clearing banks. The wheeling and dealing involved appealed to the more adventurous spirits. However, after the early inspiration of a maverick leader, the merchant banks quickly became absorbed into the mainstream establishment. In the UK there are a lot of very blue-blooded merchant bankers.

One of the oldest types of merchant banking operation – the acceptance business – was a way of lending the bank's name rather than its money – the bank was liable only if the client failed to meet its obligations. Merchant banks use their financial expertise to help their corporate clients and apart from the acceptance credits, they are active in areas like cross-border leasing (a form of international hire purchase), project finance (where a loan is tied to a particular scheme with the profits from the scheme being used to repay the loan) and factoring (where a company borrows money on the strength of its customer invoices) (see Chapter 7).

But the above activities are not the reason why merchant and investment banks are some of the most powerful players in the world financial system. Their key role is the way they link companies with capital, in the loan, bond and equity markets and in their development of new financial instruments such as derivatives (see Chapter 12).

Large companies do not rely on getting their capital in the form of loans from one or two leading banks. They have to raise funds from all over the world in a variety of forms, and thus need to get their case across to a multitude of investors.

The investment banks play the role of the middlemen in this process. They can organize a syndicated loan facility (involving a host of different banks), a bond or share issue. And if the company wants to take over a competitor, they will take charge of organizing the bid. All this comes under the portmanteau title of *corporate finance* activities.

This requires the banks to have a number of skills; first, the expertise to know what procedures have to be followed and which investors need to be contacted; second, the creativity to think of new fund-raising instruments when those are needed; third, the capital to take part in those transactions when the customer requires it.

This third element is highly important. Take a customer such as a big insurance company which wants to dispose of part of its equity portfolio very quickly. A big investment bank such as Goldman Sachs can offer to buy the position itself, counting on its ability to sell it to other investors later on.

A further need for capital stems from the fact that investment bankers often operate as market makers; they offer to buy or sell shares and bonds at a given price in the market. And the banks also act as proprietary traders, that is they speculate in the market hoping to make a profit by judging trends correctly.

That means banks need a lot of capital, something which the old smaller style UK merchant banks were unable to provide. Hence, the frequent rounds of mergers and takeovers in the industry as the UK banks concerned sought the required scale. First they teamed up with big retail banks (see Chapter 1) in the mid 1980s. The next round came in the 1990s when many of the remaining UK banks succumbed to foreign buyers: S G Warburg became part of Swiss Bank Corporation (which has since linked up with Union Bank of Switzerland); Kleinwort Benson was bought by Dresdner Bank of Germany; Barclays sold the bulk of BZW to Credit Suisse First Boston; NatWest sold much of its investment banking business to Bankers Trust of the US.

These mergers and acquisitions mean that there are very few British owned businesses operating in the investment banking industry. Some worry about the 'Wimbledonization' of London, where just as in tennis, London hosts the tournament but does not provide any of the top players.

The investment banking business is very glamorous but also very risky. Top traders can take home earnings (including their bonuses) that easily stretch into six figures and sometimes top a million. If not properly monitored, however, their activities can endanger the health of the bank, as Barings found with Nick Leeson. The new derivatives instruments, such as futures and options, that have been created in recent years, can be difficult to understand and (because they have a short track record) can behave in unpredictable ways.

Even when traders are not careless or fraudulent, they can just be wrong. When markets fall sharply, banks often face losses from their proprietary trading activities. Even the more standard activities of arranging new issues and take-overs can be highly volatile; when markets are in the doldrums, few companies use the stock market to raise capital and few bids are announced. The sudden stock market downturn in the autumn of 1998 caused a number of banks to announce one-off hits to profits.

But in the good years, the best investment banks (which tend to be in the US) can earn very high returns on capital. It is rather like the film business. A lot of films lose money and it costs a fortune to hire a

Hollywood star; but get the right picture (such as *Titanic*) and the profits are huge.

One further point is worth exploring. The biggest investment banks are all-singing, all-dancing institutions which play almost every role in the financial system. For example, many have fund management arms, which manage money on behalf of small pension funds or charities, or the savings of private investors, via unit and investment trusts.

The banks also have their own teams of investment analysts who pore through the accounts of companies listed on the market and make recommendations about which shares are attractive or overvalued.

This raises a number of conflicts of interest. Suppose a corporate finance team is arranging a takeover for a client, which involves that company using its own shares. What if the analyst covering the company thinks the shares are overvalued? That would send out a bad message to the market. But if the analyst changes his view and starts singing the praises of the shares, his clients are entitled to be cynical. And what if the company's fund management arm buys shares? Is it doing so because of a dispassionate analysis of the company's merits or because the purchase will help the deal go through?

This issue came to the fore during the dotcom boom of the late 1990s when analysts touted the attractions of companies which had never made a profit and had little even in the way of revenues.

It became clear that analysts were far from unbiased and were motivated by the need to 'do deals' – to persuade companies to hire the analyst's bank as managers for the company's flotation. The more optimistic the analysts were prepared to be, the more likely it became that his or her bank would get the deal.

Analysts face a further problem. Companies do not like to hear that their shares are overvalued, any more than actors or writers like to receive a bad review. Analysts who tell their investment clients that they should sell a company's shares may find that the company's management refuses to speak to them. That can be a real problem for an analyst seeking to prepare an in-depth report on a company's finances.

The net result of all these pressures is that analysts make very few sell recommendations – according to one survey, buy recommendations exceed sells by 9–1. Many of the big institutional investors now employ their own analysts to get round this problem of biased advice.

4

The Bank of England

The Bank of England has been, for three centuries, the centrepiece of the British financial system, an institution which in the past has been able to influence the markets with a twitch of its Governor's eyebrow. Today, having been given effective independence on monetary policy, the Bank is more important than ever.

The bank was founded back in 1694, when King William III needed money to fight Louis XIV of France. A Scottish merchant, William Paterson, suggested that a bank should be formed which could lend money to the government. Within fifteen years, the Old Lady of Threadneedle Street, as it became known, was given the monopoly of joint-stock banking in England and Wales. That ensured that it remained the biggest bank in the country since those banks which were *not* joint-stock could by law have no more than six partners, severely limiting their ability to expand. However, that monopoly was eroded by Acts in 1826 and 1833 and the Bank's pre-eminent position was not really cemented until the Bank Charter Act of 1844. The Act followed a succession of banking failures, which was blamed on the overissue of banknotes. Until 1844, any bank had the right to issue its own notes, opening up the risk not only of fraud but also of inflation. The Bank Charter Act restricted the rights of banks other than the Bank of England to issue notes, a restriction which became total (in England and Wales) in 1921. Scottish banks can still print notes.

By that time, the Bank's position as one of the country's most prestigious institutions had been established and the inter-war governor, Montagu Norman, was one of the most influential men of his age. Such was the power of the Old Lady that the Attlee government thought it right to nationalize it in 1946.

The election of the Labour government in May 1997 ushered in a new phase in the Bank's history. One of the first acts of the Chancellor, Gordon Brown, was to give the Bank the power to set interest rates. Now every month, traders wait anxiously to see what the Bank has decided.

Gordon Brown's decision owed a lot to the rather unhappy history of UK economic policy during the war. Britain suffered from a much higher rate of inflation than many of its competitors and the pound endured a seemingly relentless decline (see Chapter 13).

Many people felt that one reason for the country's poor performance was the control that politicians exercised over interest rates. When inflation was starting to pick up, politicians proved reluctant to raise rates, especially if a general election was in sight, because of the unpopularity with the voters that would be caused.

In theory, a central bank, consisting of 'dispassionate' professionals who did not have to face the electorate would not face the same pressures. Economists noted that independent central banks in the US (the Federal Reserve) and Germany (the Bundesbank) had been much more successful in controlling inflation.

For a time, under the Conservative government of 1992–97, a hybrid system was in place in which the Chancellor met the Bank of England Governor every month and the former then made a rate decision, based on the latter's advice. Although the minutes of the meetings were published in a bid to create transparency, the system was not entirely successful; when the Governor proposed rate increases in the run-up to the 1997 election, the then Chancellor Kenneth Clarke turned him down.

The new system means that the Governor of the Bank is an extremely important person, with the effective power to set our mortgage rates. The current occupant, Sir Edward George, was promoted from within the Bank's ranks after the retirement of Robin Leigh-Pemberton and was appointed to a second five-year term in February 1998.

But the Bank's new interest rate powers have been offset by a substantial loss of influence elsewhere. The Bank no longer supervises the banking system – that role has been transferred to a new regulator called the Financial Services Authority (see Chapter 15). And the Bank's role in controlling the UK government debt market – deciding when to make new issues or smooth out fluctuations in the market – is being transferred to a new body. The Bank still, however, has the responsibility for printing new banknotes. The earliest notes were handwritten on Bank paper and were payable for precise sums in pounds, shillings and pence. More standard notes were introduced in the eighteenth century. The appearance of the Queen's head on notes, a subject which caused recent controversy when it was suggested that it would vanish with the advent of a single currency, did not occur until 1960.

The Bank produces around 1.3 billion notes a year, at an average cost of 3 pence each; the £10 note is the most popular with over 600m (or £6bn worth) issued in 1997. Before the phasing out of £1 notes, the Bank was printing 7.5 million new notes every day (and withdrawing around the same number). That was equal to around thirty new notes per year for every person in the country. British people are notoriously unwilling to handle old banknotes; in Germany only nine new notes are printed per person per year.

The watermark and the metal bar are not the only reasons why notes are difficult to forge; the hand-engraved portraits and intricate geometric patterns are also extremely difficult to reproduce. As from January 1999, the signature on the bottom of banknotes became that of Merlyn Lowther, the Bank's chief cashier, who is the first woman of the 29 people to hold the post since 1694.

Another duty which the Bank retains is for the overall health of the UK financial system. This remains an extremely important role, since technically it enables the Bank to set the level of interest rates throughout the economy.

The Bank is the 'lender of last resort' for the banking system, that is, the institution to whom the private sector banks can turn when they are short of cash.

This does not mean that the Bank is forever stepping in to rescue banks. But banks lend and borrow on a daily basis in the money markets (see Chapter 5), and often there are imbalances (more people want to lend than borrow or vice versa). The Bank steps in to supply credit (lend money) when there is a shortage.

The rate that the Bank charges for this facility is effectively the base cost that banks must pay. It was known for a long time as the base rate, or the minimum lending rate. Nowadays, for complicated reasons explained in the next chapter, it is known as the repo rate, but the effect is the same.

In a few cases, the Bank may have to help out in a more serious way, if it becomes clear that a financial institution is in danger of going bust. It organized a rescue package for Johnson Matthey in 1984, for example, but found it could not do so when Barings got into trouble.

A banking failure of one of the big high street banks would cause enormous problems in the financial system. Customers would start to distrust all banks, withdraw their money and force banks to ask for the repayment of loans by their borrowers. The resulting credit crunch could force the economy into depression, as was the case after 1929. The mere knowledge that the Bank of England is there as a source of potential support gives investors greater confidence in the financial system.

THE MONETARY POLICY COMMITTEE

How does the Bank actually make its decision on setting interest rates? Gordon Brown created a monetary policy committee which consists of nine people, five from within the Bank and four from outside. The four outsiders have so far been economists with an academic background, with the notable exception of DeAnne Julius who was an economist at British Airways and her successor Kate Barker, who was chief economist at the Confederation of British Industry.

The committee meets, normally on the second Wednesday and Thursday of each month, and announces its decision at noon on the second day.

The Bank makes a fair attempt to make the process transparent. The minutes of the meeting are published two weeks later, with details of how each member of the committee actually voted.

Every quarter, the Bank publishes an inflation report, which reviews the progress made in combating inflation and forecasts the likely level of inflation over the next two years. And the Bank also has to come to Parliament to explain its actions to MPs.

These actions help deflect the criticism that the unelected central bankers are running the economy without reference to the concerns of ordinary people. Attacks on the Bank were particularly marked in June 1998 when it raised rates to 7.5 per cent at a time when the manufacturing sector was already struggling under the weight of a strong pound. It was noted then that DeAnne Julius, the sole member of the committee with experience in industry, was the only one to vote against the move.

But so far there has been little sign of the Bank members 'ganging up' on the minority of outsiders. Indeed, sometimes the five Bank representatives have voted in opposite directions.

The target set by the Chancellor for the Bank is to keep the inflation rate at 2.5 per cent; the Governor is required to send a letter of explanation should the rate deviate by more than 1 percentage point on either side of this target. The aim is to avoid either excessive inflation or deflation, a state of falling prices which is normally associated with economic contraction.

The rate targeted is the underlying rate of inflation, which excludes mortgage interest payments. This may seem a bit of a fiddle; most of us have mortgages and thus a rise in the interest rate reflects an increase in our cost of living.

But if the Bank were to include mortgage payments, it would face a paradox. Every time it increased rates to target inflation, the effect would be a rise in inflation itself. By stripping out mortgages, it can have a clearer picture of what is going on in the underlying economy.

The Bank has another measure which strips out the effect of tax rises such as increases in alcohol or tobacco duties, since they too can distort the real picture.

The committee members pay attention to factors such as commodity costs, wage rises, the strength or weakness of the pound and money supply growth in setting rates. So far, it has had reasonable success with both inflation and interest rates staying much lower than they did in the 1970s and 1980s.

THE BANK'S LONG-TERM FUTURE

The Bank of England's new power over interest rates may be short-lived. Much depends on whether the UK decides to become part of the European single currency, the euro.

At the time of writing, the government was still in the process of assessing five economic tests which would determine whether euro entry was in the UK's best interest. Even if the tests are passed, a referendum will be held – and opinion polls indicate that British opinion is firmly against the single currency.

But if all the hurdles were cleared, the European Central Bank, based in Frankfurt, would become the body that determined UK interest rates with the Bank of England reduced to a local regulatory role.

The ECB sets one interest rate for the whole of Europe, based on its understanding of continent wide inflation pressures. This creates the possibility that, if inflation is rampant in, say, Ireland, little will be done to combat the problem if prices are stable in the core countries of France and Germany.

That will mean that the UK will lack either of its well-worn tactics for climbing out of recession – devaluing the pound or cutting interest rates – if it joins up for the single currency. And those industrialists who complain about remote City bankers now will have to address their concerns to Frankfurt.

5

The Money Markets

The primary aim of most financial institutions is quite simple. They need to borrow money more cheaply than they can lend it. The most obvious illustration of this principle is the commercial banks. They receive a substantial amount of their funds in current accounts, which pay no or a reduced amount of interest but from which the funds may be withdrawn at any moment. They lend out such funds at market rates of interest. Because depositors can demand their money immediately, the banks want to keep a substantial proportion of their money in liquid form. This they do by lending it to other financial institutions in the so-called money markets.

Banks can also find themselves short of the cash needed to meet their obligations and thus have to *borrow* in the money markets. The markets are therefore one of the main channels through which banks can iron out day-to-day fluctuations in their cash flow. For the investment banks, the money markets are a very important source of funds for their dealings since they do not possess the customer deposits of the clearing banks. To distinguish them from the retail markets, the money markets are often known as the *wholesale markets* and the deposits or bills involved are usually denominated in large amounts. A typical deal might involve a loan of tens of millions of pounds.

Transactions in the money markets have traditionally been in the form of either deposits or bills. Deposits are made (with the exception of money-at-call) for set periods of time at an agreed rate of interest. Bills are pieces of paper which are issued at a discount to their face value. The bills can then be traded by their holders after issue.

The practice of discounting bills was the main activity of a group of institutions called the discount houses. The discount houses were for a long time the main link between the Bank of England and the money markets.

THE MONEY MARKETS

What instruments are traded in the money markets? The best known is probably the Treasury bill, although its importance varies with the government's financing needs. In the 1970s, the Treasury's weekly offer was sometimes over £500 million. In the 1980s, the figure dropped to around £100 million a week.

As a result, commercial bills became a much more important part of the money market. These can be bills in the real sense, referring to some specific commercial transaction. The customer gives the supplier an IOU; the supplier sells it to a financial institution for less than its face value in order to get the money in advance. When the customer eventually pays up, whoever holds the bill gets the money. However, commercial bills are often not related to any particular business deal. They are just one more means of borrowing money.

Nowadays, companies are quite sophisticated about their methods of raising finance. If commercial bill rates fall below other interest rates, this can lead to the process known as 'roundtripping'. This occurs when companies borrow by issuing commercial bills and invest the proceeds in the money markets, making a guaranteed profit in the process.

As well as commercial bills, many companies borrow money in the form of commercial paper. Commercial paper facilities can extend to the hundreds of millions of pounds and are used by companies to fund their short-term financing needs, such as acquisitions.

In addition to Treasury and commercial bills, another widely used instrument in the money markets is the certificate of deposit. The simplest definition of a certificate of deposit (CD) is that it is a tradeable document attesting that the holder has lent money to a bank or building society.

CDs are a highly important form of investment in the money markets. If an investor puts his or her money into a term loan, it cannot be withdrawn until the loan matures. A CD, however, can be sold by an investor if the funds are needed suddenly. They are dealt with on an interest-accrued basis (i.e. the money that the CD would have earned is added to the CD's face value). However, the rate which the investor will effectively have earned will depend on the way that interest rates have moved since the CD was purchased.

For example, an investor buys a three-month CD for £100,000 at an interest rate of 10 per cent. If the CD is held until maturity, the bank would repay the investor £102,500.* That sum will be repaid to whoever holds the CD when it matures. After a month, the investor decides to sell the CD. Its price will not necessarily be one-third of the way between £100,000 and £102,500 (i.e. £100,833); it will be so only if interest rates have stabilized and if investors expect interest rates to stay at 10 per cent. If rates have dropped (or are expected to drop), the price will be more than £100,833 because it will be more attractive to other investors. If rates have risen (or are expected to rise), then the price will be less than £100,833 because investors will be able to get more attractive interest rates elsewhere. In either case, the price will settle at the level where it is equivalent to other prevailing market rates.

In return for receiving the extra liquidity that the CD provides, investors are ready to accept a slightly lower interest rate than on the equivalent term deposit. Borrowers (which are mostly banks) get the benefit of the slightly lower interest rate and are still guaranteed that the money will not have to be repaid until the CD matures.

CDs may be issued for periods up to five years and are normally issued in amounts ranging from £50,000 to £500,000. In the UK, the size of an individual certificate is at least £10,000. In the USA, however, they have been issued in smaller denominations in order to attract individual investors.

Another component of the money markets are gilt-edged securities near the end of their life. Since the gilts are about to be repaid, they start to resemble the other instruments prevailing in the markets.

All these instruments share a feature noted in the Introduction to this book – their price changes when interest rates move. If short-term interest rates fall, then CDs, etc., which pay a higher rate, will be more valuable and will rise in price. If interest rates rise, then the price of previously issued instruments will fall. Conversely, those who (like the discount

---

* A year's interest would be £10,000. Divide by four to get the three-month figure of £2,500.

houses) invest in the money markets tend to hope for interest rates to fall, since they then make a capital gain on their investments.

In 1996, a new element was added to the money markets, the gilt repo. These are short term agreements, whereby borrowers use government bonds (gilts) as collateral for loans. The development of this practice, which had been in existence in the US for some time, added liquidity to the gilts market and widened the number of institutions with which the Bank of England could deal.

Shortly afterwards, the Bank moved to make the repo one of its main tools for intervening in the money markets. By varying the rate it charges banks for lending against gilts, it can affect the level of interest rates charged throughout the economy. Hence, the key UK interest rates which used to be known as the base, or minimum lending, rate is now known as the repo rate.

Not all instruments in the money market are tradeable. Local authority loans form one of the oldest sectors of the money markets. Lending money to local authorities is a steady and unspectacular business but the 1980s storms over ratecapping highlighted the fact that local authorities can look to the City for funds.

THE PLAYERS IN THE MARKETS

The bulk of the activity in the markets consists of banks borrowing and lending to and from each other, sometimes with the assistance of a broker. Most of the loans have maturities of three months or less.

Much of this trading takes place via the telephone, with traders watching market prices move on electronic screens. Each trader will be seeking to manage the bank's money for profit. He or she will attempt to do so in one of two ways. As in the foreign-exchange markets (see Chapter 13), dealers charge a spread between rates. They will lend at a slightly higher rate than the rate at which they will borrow. The spread may be as small as $1/_{32}$ of a percentage point. Because of the size of the deals involved, the cumulative effect of spreads can add up to a sizeable profit.

However, the dealer cannot rely on the spread alone. Interest rates are constantly fluctuating. This can wipe out the dealer's spread. For example, a dealer may agree to lend at $8\,1/_{32}$ per cent and borrow at 8 per cent. He accordingly lends money at $8\,^1/_{32}$ per cent. While he is making the deal, the market moves to $8\,^1/_8$–$8\,^3/_{32}$ per cent. If the dealer now borrows the money the bank needs to cover the loan, he or she will now have to pay $8\,^3/_{32}$ per cent, $^2/_{32}$ per cent more than the bank is receiving, even allowing for the spread.

The second way that money market dealers make money, therefore, is by trying to anticipate these moves in rates. If they expect rates to rise, they will borrow more than they lend (in market parlance, 'go short'). If they expect rates to fall, they will lend more than they borrow ('go long'). So in the above example, the dealer went long at the wrong time – when markets were rising. Had he or she gone short and borrowed at 8 per cent, then when rates rose the dealer could have lent the bank's money at the new higher rate.

MONEY BROKERS

Linking the activities of the money market dealers are the money brokers. They wheel and deal on the telephone, linking lenders and borrowers in return for a commission. Unlike the dealers, they do not lend and borrow themselves. They depend on high turnover to make money. Fortunately for the brokers, turnover has grown considerably over the past few years as interest rates have fluctuated more violently. The commission the brokers earn is tiny (less than 0.02 per cent). However, all those small percentages add up to a lot of money when the principal sums involved are so large. Even the advent of negotiated commissions at the start of 1986 did not prevent the larger brokers from maintaining their profits.

The real importance of the money markets is that they react very sensitively to economic changes. Rates will rise very quickly if, for example, dealers think that inflation is increasing or that the pound is about to fall. Foreign investors can quickly withdraw their funds if they are worried about the UK economy. The flight of this so-called 'hot money' can put real pressure on a government.

So far, our coverage of financial institutions has focused only on banks. In the next chapter, we shall look at a rival set of institutions, the building societies.

6 Building Societies

Building societies face a threat to their long-term survival. Now that a number of the biggest societies have opted to become banks (see Chapter 3), many wonder whether Britain needs building societies at all.

For a long time, however, societies were perceived as one of the most consumer friendly elements of the financial system. They were the repositories of the small savings of millions of people and the providers of finance for the vast majority of home purchases. Few folded because of financial mismanagement.

Societies have grown closer and closer to banks in any case. In the old days, they talked of surpluses, now they talk of profits. They compete with banks in terms of offering current accounts, cheque books, cashpoint cards, personal loans, foreign exchange, unit trusts and life assurance.

Only in structure are they different. Societies are mutual societies, owned by their members (savers), rather than public companies with shareholders.

ORIGINS

The original building societies were literally that – groups of individuals who subscribed to a common fund so that they could buy or build themselves a house. Once the house or group of houses were built, the societies were folded up.

After a rather shaky period in the late nineteenth century, when a spate of society collapses sapped public confidence in the movement, the building societies have established an important place in the financial community.

The scramble for personal savings increased in the 1980s when the Building Societies Association's control over the mortgage and savings rates charged by members gradually weakened. The result was that building societies began to compete more aggressively among themselves for funds, with extra interest accounts offering instant withdrawal without penalty for the saver. The proportion of building society deposits obtained from ordinary share accounts fell from 90 per cent in 1974 to less than 10 per cent at the end of 1987. Most depositors now hold savings in stepped accounts, which gradually increase the interest rate as the amount of savings rises. The highest rates of return can be obtained in accounts with certain restrictions – notice may be needed for withdrawals, for example.

THE MORTGAGE BUSINESS

As noted in the Introduction, building societies perform a piece of financial magic by turning customers' deposits, which can be withdrawn at any time, into home loans, extending up to thirty-five years. To guard against sudden shortfalls in deposits, they also have limited investments in safe short-term instruments like short-dated gilts. For much of the twentieth century, the business of building societies was extremely sound because of the credit record of its borrowers. Most people made every effort they could to keep up the payments on their mortgage; and since inflation tended to erode the value of the debt, it was relatively easy for them to do so.

But the 1980s saw a house price bubble. The profits made by some people in the housing market and tax incentives designed to encourage home ownership drew more and more people into the housing market. Competition from other lenders caused building societies to lower their credit requirements; many people were allowed to buy homes on 100 per cent loans, that is without putting up a deposit, and were lent large sums in proportion to their incomes.

All this activity was built on the assumption that house prices would rise forever. But the bubble eventually burst, as all bubbles do. High interest rates weakened borrowers' ability to pay and falling house prices meant that the mortgages became worth more than the homes – what became known as 'negative equity' (see Chapter 14).

Societies were faced with a tricky dilemma. Once borrowers default on their interest payments, societies have the right to reclaim the asset, i.e. the house. But selling the house would not provide enough cash to pay off the loan. Furthermore, the more homes the societies repossessed, the more empty homes there were on the property market, depressing house prices and giving an extra twist to the downward spiral.

The long-term prospects for the building societies were blighted by a change in government policy. Politicians finally recognized that the British obsession with home ownership had not been great news for the economy. Tax relief on mortgage interest, in particular, was an excessive subsidy to the middle class. Chancellors in the 1990s accordingly whittled away the tax relief, initially reducing the maximum rate at which it applied and then abolishing it altogether.

There was a flurry of money into building societies in the mid 1990s as investors realized the potential windfall gains that could be made when societies converted into banks. But since this rather resembled the flurry of vultures round a starving animal, this was hardly an encouraging long-term sign for the industry.

A SHRINKING INDUSTRY

Even before the wave of mergers in the mid 1990s, the industry had experienced a long period of consolidation. The total number of societies fell from 2,286 in 1900 to 273 in 1980 and 67 by late 2001. The smallest societies are still pretty tiny; the largest, Nationwide, had £46bn of assets in 1998, while the smallest had just £11m.

The principles that applied in many other industries applied to the societies. Economies of scale helped societies reduce costs and that enabled them to offer better rates, pull in more depositors and achieve greater economies of scale.

But greater size brought its own dangers. At the start of the 1980s, building societies were still very small compared with the big banks, but their success encouraged banks to enter the mortgage market. Competition between the banks and the societies became intense and has remained so now that many former societies have converted.

Increased competition in the mortgage market meant that societies had to look elsewhere for profits. Mortgages now come with a lot of bells and whistles attached. In the 1980s, there was a big drive to sell endowment mortgages, loans linked to an insurance policy which would grow sufficiently (in theory) to repay the capital. Endowments earned high commissions for the societies. In the 1990s, as endowments have become less popular, attention has switched to building and contents insurance.

In the savings market, competition has forced societies to abandon some of their long-held customs. In November 1984, the Building Societies Association Council decided to stop recommending specific interest rates to its members, bringing an end to the interest-rate cartel which the societies had practised for so long. The resulting competition has led societies to increase the number of so-called 'premium' accounts which grant savers extra interest if they fulfil certain conditions. They have also attacked the banks head on by offering withdrawals from automated teller machines, chequing facilities and home banking. The latter developments, as we have already seen, have had profound effects on UK monetary policy.

The twin phenomena of competition in raising money from depositors and competition in mortgage lending increased societies' costs and put pressure on their revenues. The amount received from depositors each month has been subject to violent fluctuations, particularly during waves of privatizations.

Societies are now also able to make good any shortfalls in their deposits by borrowing in the main financial markets. They have issued certificates of deposit and borrowed in the Euromarkets. The societies have also found a new source of capital in the form of 'Permanent Interest Bearing Shares', which are effectively a type of bond which will never be repaid.

THE MORTGAGE RATE

So what determines whether the mortgage rate goes up or down? More than ever before, it is the general level of rates in the economy. The building societies cannot stay separate from the other financial institutions, since they must compete with them for depositors and they must sometimes borrow from them. As the cost of raising their funds rises and falls, so must the mortgage rate. In general, however, the mortgage rate is slower both to rise and to fall than bank rates.

As interest rates rise and fall, societies switch their concern between savers and borrowers. In 1990, when base rates were 15 per cent, the typical mortgage rate was just a fraction above that level, at 15.4 per cent. Societies were holding down the rate to prevent any more pain being inflicted on homeowners. In late 2001, when the Bank of England cut rates to 4 per cent, many building societies were charging 5.5 per cent, a margin of 1.5 percentage points. The societies had switched their concern from borrowers to savers.

A big change in the 1990s came with the development of fixed rate mortgages. These promise borrowers a set rate for several years at a time, allowing them to plan their budgets and avoid the danger of a sudden jump in rates. The catch is that borrowers do not benefit if rates fall and, if they try to repay the loan ahead of time, they face heavy redemption penalties.

Building societies fund fixed rate deals by borrowing long term and as we saw in Chapter 2, the yield curve means that long rates are normally different from short rates. Sometimes, as in 1998, long-term interest rates are well below short rates and this means fixed rate deals are below conventional rates; making it a very good time to get a fix.

Chapter 2 has already described some of the theories of interest-rate movements. However, it is important to remember that rates can rise for reasons external to this country – as a response to a run on sterling by overseas investors, for example.

THE URGE TO CONVERT

The drive for conversion really began in the 1980s. As the competition between banks and building societies increased, some societies complained about the restrictions placed upon them. The most onerous requirement, in their opinion, was that building society lending was restricted to the mortgage of freehold and leasehold property in the UK. Some societies wanted to widen their business to compete even further with banks, in the way that their US equivalents, the savings and loans institutions (S&Ls), had done. The fact that many S&Ls ran into financial difficulties in the process did not deter the bolder building societies. They argued, with some justification, that the problem which hit US S&Ls was that their investments were in fixed rate mortgages which were left behind, as interest rates rose, by the increased costs of the S&Ls' borrowings. In the UK, there was, until recently, little use of fixed rate mortgages – if interest rates rise, so does the return from the building societies' investments.

THE 1986 BUILDING SOCIETIES ACT

The then Conservative government recognized that the societies had some cause for complaint. It had an ideological commitment to increasing competition in the financial markets. In 1986 it accordingly passed the Building Societies Act which was designed to allow societies to expand the range of their activities.

Under the legislation, societies were allowed to devote 15 per cent of their lending to so-called Class 3 assets, which cover unsecured loans and other activities such as residential property investment and investments in estate agencies, insurance brokers and other subsidiary activities. Up to 10 per cent could be devoted to Class 2 assets, which cover second mortgages, equity mortgages and other secured lending. However, at least 85 per cent of the total portfolio had to be devoted to first mortgages to owner-occupiers. A newly formed body, the Building Society Commission, was allowed to raise the ceilings but only to 20 per cent for Class 2 and 10 per cent for Class 3. Societies were able to raise 20 per cent of their funds from the wholesale (i.e. money) markets. Once again, the Commission had the power to raise this level from 20 per cent to 40 per cent.

Most importantly, the Act gave societies the freedom to become limited companies. However, there were various restrictions on this freedom. A society could become a company only if the move were approved by 75 per cent of voting investors, 50 per cent of voting borrowers and 20 per cent of all investors.

Societies that have converted, which have included Abbey National, Alliance & Leicester, the Halifax, Northern Rock and the Woolwich, have tended to distribute free shares to their savers and borrowers. That has created an artificial shortage in the market, as investment institutions, such as pension funds, scramble to get their allocation of stock and bid prices higher.

The result has been a bonanza for building society members which has put pressure on other societies to convert. The Nationwide, the largest remaining society, narrowly fought off a call for conversion in the summer of 1998.

Other societies have seen the arrival of 'carpet-baggers' – savers who have deposited small sums in a number of institutions in the hope of benefiting from a spate of windfalls. Many societies have put up barricades, such as minimum investment levels, to prevent carpet-baggers cashing in.

The Act allows one society that wants to take over another to appeal directly to its members, over the heads of the target society's management. However, the bidder has to wait three months before it can gain access to the list of the target society's members. In addition, a society which becomes a company is partially protected against predators. No one investor will be able to hold more than 15 per cent of the shares, and takeover bids would be subject to the rules of the Takeover Panel. So far, the most prominent takeover was of Cheltenham & Gloucester by Lloyds Bank.

Enthusiasts for the sector still hope that it can survive. The principle of mutuality is highly attractive but somewhere in the recent history of the movement, it rather lost its way; few members bothered to vote on society matters and managers seemed more interested in expanding their organizations (thereby increasing their power and salaries) than in genuinely looking after the interests of their members.

A prime example was when some societies changed the structure of their savings accounts, stranding some savers in low-paying vehicles, without informing their members in writing. That did not enhance their reputation for consumer friendliness.

There are some hopeful signs. A new Building Societies Act, passed in 1997, should give the remaining societies greater freedom to move into new areas of business. If societies can pay rigorous attention to the interests of their members by keeping down their costs, offering competitive rates to savers and borrowers, and by refusing to sell unsuitable add-on policies just because it earns them commission, then there should be a place for them in the twenty-first century financial system.

Borrowers

The financial institutions described in the last few chapters play the function in the economy of channelling funds from those who wish to lend to those who wish to borrow. In the next two chapters we will look at the lenders and the borrowers. There are three main groups of borrowers in the economy: individuals, governments and companies. The job of the financial system is to channel funds to those borrowers from investors. Of course, in playing that role, banks and other financial intermediaries must both borrow and invest. However, this chapter examines those borrowers who are not financial institutions, and the alternatives open to them.

INDIVIDUALS

Individuals borrow for a host of different reasons. Perhaps the most common is that income and expenditure are rarely synchronized. Christmas comes but once a year but drives many people into overdraft. Few people can afford to buy larger consumer durables (like washing machines) without borrowing the funds involved. Unplanned events such as illness or redundancy can reduce income without a corresponding effect on expenditure. Food must still be bought and rent and mortgages must be paid.

Most people borrow by taking out an overdraft from a bank or carrying a credit-card balance. Banks will also lend money for more specific projects, like study courses or home improvements. Finance companies and big businesses will lend money to those buying expensive goods. However, the most important debt which most people incur is to buy a home with a mortgage.

GOVERNMENTS

British governments have historically spent more than their incomes and, like anyone else, they have to borrow to cover the difference. They borrow in the form of long-dated securities called gilts and short-dated securities called Treasury bills. Money is also borrowed direct from the public through the various national savings schemes on offer (see Chapter 14). The government can give itself a built-in advantage in the market for personal savings because it can allow savers to escape tax. It does so on some schemes. However, the loss of tax income increases the government's cost of borrowing. As a result, it tries to maintain a balance between the amount it borrows in the form of savings schemes, bills and gilts.

The total amount that most governments have had to borrow has increased in post-war years, because of the growth of welfare economies in the West with the resulting inbuilt increases in expenditure. Few governments have been willing to take the unpopular step of raising taxes to cut the deficit. The expenditure side of the equation has suffered accordingly. The result in the UK has been continuous battles over cuts in spending between those ministries with escalating budgets (particularly the Departments of Health, Social Security, Environment and Defence) and the Treasury.

The difference between the government's total revenue and its expenditure is known as the public-sector borrowing requirement (PSBR) or more recently the Public Sector Net Cash Requirement. Reducing this deficit was one of the main aims of the Conservative government of 1979–97.

In the early days of Mrs Thatcher's administration, the economic rationale behind the government's desire to reduce the PSBR was that a fall in government borrowing would stimulate the economy. If the PSBR is too high, it was reasoned, the available funds for investment will flow to the government (a safe credit) rather than to industry. Companies will be able to borrow only by offering investors penally high rates of interest, discouraging them from investing in new plant and machinery. Without new investment, the economy will not grow. The government will effectively have 'crowded out' private-sector borrowing. A low PSBR, the government argued, would result in low interest rates. Businesses would be encouraged to invest and the economy would grow.

The drive to cut government deficits spread more widely in the 1980s and 1990s. The heavy defence expenditure incurred by the US during the cold war had caused its deficit to rise sharply. Tax rises and some spending cuts imposed by Presidents Bush and Clinton helped bring down the shortfall in the 1990s.

In Europe, an annual deficit of less than 3 per cent of gross domestic product was one of the key 'Maastricht convergence criteria' that countries had to meet in order to qualify for the single currency. Governments duly cut back, albeit with the help of some dodgy accounting tricks.

This attention to deficits owes something to a general realization by politicians that running up debts on the never-never is a short-sighted strategy. Gradually, interest payments on previous debts consume an increasing proportion of the annual budget.

And the rise of the so-called 'bond market vigilantes' has also made it more difficult for profligate governments. Countries have to raise money from the international markets and in these days of free capital flows, investors will be quick to sell the government bonds of a nation if it suspects its finances are deteriorating. That will increase the cost of raising new money and make the government's finances even worse.

There are no easy exits. If a country's position gets really bad, it will be forced to go to the International Monetary Fund for help – but the IMF will impose tough conditions in terms of spending cutbacks and tax rises. The option of default – refusing to pay the nation's debts – will cut the country off from international capital for a long time, and lead to further economic hardship.

The bonds issued by the UK government are called *gilt-edged securities*, or gilts, because of the near certainty that they will be repaid.

They fall into three categories, conventional, index-linked and the irredeemables. Conventional gilts pay a fixed rate of interest twice a year and have repayment dates varying from five to 30 years.

Index-linked gilts pay a low rate of interest (2 to 4 per cent) but this interest, and the repayment value of the bonds, is linked to the retail price index. If prices double over the lifetime of the bond, then those who bought when the bond was first issued will be repaid twice their original investment.

Irredeemable issues are a bit of a historical throwback. They are literally issues that will not be repaid. Some were issued in the nineteenth century on very low rates of interest and now trade well below their face value. But their yield (the interest rate divided by the face value) is at around the same level as other issues in the market. Examples of irredeemables include Consols and War Loan.

A new type of gilts trading has also been introduced, called *strips*. Under a strip, a gilt issue is separated into a series of different payments; all the interest payments between now and the repayment date and the final repayment value. These separate units offer an interesting investment opportunity; they have a certain final value but pay no income in the interim. They can be useful for tax planning (see Chapter 14).

Of course, the UK government bond market is not the largest in the world. By far the biggest, and most important, is the US Treasury bond market. Even though the US has had a long-running tendency to budget deficits, its government bonds are the most liquid and are seen as a 'safe haven' when other markets are in turmoil. The Japanese government bond market is also important, and notable in the late 1990s for temporarily offering yields of less than 1 per cent; the European bond market may eventually rival the US once the single currency becomes established.

COMPANIES

Why do companies borrow? Unlike individuals, for whom borrowing is often a sign of financial weakness, borrowing is a way of life for most corporations, no matter what their prospects. Firms which are very successful often have substantial amounts of debt. There obviously comes a point beyond which companies can be said to have borrowed too much, but frequently, corporate borrowing merely indicates a willingness to expand.

What routes are open to a company which wishes to finance expansion? It might be imagined that the ideal method would be to generate the funds from past profits (retained earnings). In other words, the company would finance itself and thus reduce its costs by avoiding interest payments. However, self-financing is not always possible. While companies are in their early years, they have little in the way of previous profits to draw on, since many of their investors will not yet have generated a return. Nevertheless, in order to establish themselves, companies must continue to invest in further projects, necessitating capital outlay. If they were forced to wait until funds were available internally, they might miss profitable opportunities and spoil their long-term prospects in the process. Company results are often judged by their profitability in relation to their equity base (the value of the combined shareholdings). Debt can be used to increase the return on equity (a process known as *leverage* or *gearing*) by allowing companies to seek profitable investment opportunities when retained earnings are insufficient.

Another way that a company could generate cash for expansion would be to sell existing assets or alternatively not to replace old and worn-out assets. Both, however, are one-off ways of raising money and are more indicative of a company which is winding down than of one which is expanding.

A company could increase its capital base by issuing new shares or equity. However, it might not wish to do so because that would weaken the control of the existing shareholders. In companies where control is exercised by a small majority of shareholders' votes, that could be particularly important.

It is also possible for a company to have too much equity. It is in the nature of equity (see Chapter 9) that, unlike debt, it cannot be redeemed. If the company issued more equity and then failed to expand, it would be left with large cash balances. Paying those balances back to shareholders in the form of increased dividends would have severe tax disadvantages.

In the 1990s, many companies moved to return cash to shareholders by buying back their own shares, rather than paying dividends. This had the effect of pushing up share prices (the same level of demand was chasing a smaller supply) and was one of the factors behind the long bull market.

Often companies borrowed money to finance the buyback of shares. Debt, as a financing technique, has some distinct advantages. Interest is tax-deductible from company profits, so the effective cost of borrowing is reduced. In addition, debt is reversible. If a company finds itself flush with cash or lacking in investment opportunities, it can repay some of its borrowings. Most shareholders will accept the need for a company to borrow, provided that they expect that the project in which the borrowed funds will be invested will yield a higher return than the cost of borrowing the funds. As already noted, a company can be described as being inefficient if it achieves a very low return on equity – borrowing can increase that return.

Company analysts tend to watch the debt–equity ratio, which is very roughly defined as the company's borrowings and its shareholders' funds. Ideal debt–equity ratios vary from industry to industry, but most companies start to look a little exposed if their debt exceeds their equity capital – in other words, if the ratio is larger than 1.

HOW COMPANIES OBTAIN EXTRA FINANCE

Which are the debt instruments most used by companies? The overdraft is probably still the most common method of borrowing for small firms. The overdraft has built-in advantages – it is very flexible and easy to understand. An upper limit is agreed by the bank and the borrower: the borrower may borrow any amount up to that limit but will be charged interest only on the amount outstanding at any one time. The rate charged will be agreed at a set margin over the bank's base rate and thus the cost of the overdraft will move up and down with the general level of rates in the economy.

The overdraft is a very British institution. In the US, it is virtually unknown. There companies borrow term loans – the amount and duration of which are agreed in advance – and interest is charged on the full amount for the full period of the loan.

Companies have found that the 'hard core' element of their overdrafts has increased over the years, suggesting that they are funding their long-term needs with short-term loans. Accordingly, many companies have begun to switch to funding with term loans from banks instead of overdrafts. Term loans are normally granted by banks for specific purposes such as the acquisition of machinery, property or another company, rather than for the financing of working capital needs such as the payment of wages or raw-material costs.

Overdraft financing was probably the only source of funding for the smaller companies up to twenty years ago. Many companies now borrow in the money markets, often using the services of a money broker to find a willing lender, which is likely to be a bank. In return, the broker (who never lends or borrows money himself) receives a commission. Money-market loans are for set amounts and periods and are therefore less flexible than overdraft facilities. However, interest rates in the money markets are generally below those for overdrafts.

Larger companies borrow hundreds of millions, or even billions, of pounds from groups of banks in the form of syndicated loans or loan facilities (see Chapter 10).

Longer-term finance for large firms is most frequently obtained by the issue of bonds which pay a fixed rate of interest to the investor. Such bonds usually have maturities of over five years. Multi-national firms which have very large financing needs may turn to the international and Eurobond markets (see Chapter 10). Those markets give firms access to a very wide investor base and allow companies to raise tens of millions of pounds at a stroke.

The more sophisticated financing techniques of the Euromarkets are not open to the small and medium-sized British firm. Their long-term financing needs are normally satisfied by some kind of bank loan. However, there are a variety of options open to firms seeking shorter-term finance. One in particular is the acceptance credit or banker's acceptance. A bank agrees that it will accept bills drawn on it by the company, in return for a commission. When the company needs funds, it will send the bills to the bank, which will then discount them – that is, pay the company less than the full amount of their value. The amount of discount is equivalent to the rate of interest charged by the bank. So, if the company sent the bank a three-month bill with a face value of £100 and the interest rate on such bills was 12 per cent a year, the bank would discount the bill to £97.* As with other loans, the credit rating of the company will affect the cost of the borrowing: the poorer the credit rating, the bigger the discount.

---

* Because it is a three-month bill, the discount is a quarter of the full year's rate.

THE FINANCING OF TRADE

Many of the more specialist methods of raising finance revolve around the financing of trade. The key principles are that it is better to be paid by debtors as soon as possible and pay creditors as late as possible. It is also important to ensure that debtors settle their debts. This is a particular problem for exporters who are dealing with customers out of reach of the UK legal system.

There are four main methods of payment for exports:* (1) cash with order; (2) open account trading; (3) bills of exchange; (4) documentary letters of credit.

The best method for the exporter is cash with order. That way the exporting company already has the money before it sends off the goods; however, importers can obviously not be so keen to pay by this method and it is rarely used. Open account trading is the opposite end of the scale – the exporter sends the client the goods and then waits for the cheques to arrive. It offers the least security of all the payment methods but is still the most widely used, at least in trade between industrialized countries.

Bills of exchange offer rather more security to the exporter. The firm will send the bill ('draw' it) to its foreign customer with the invoices and the necessary official documentation (referred to as a *documentary bill*). Then the firm will inform its bank, telling it to obtain the cash from the client. The bank will send the documentary bill to a bank in the importer's country. Under some arrangements, the buyer pays for the goods as soon as he receives the documents. Often, however, he is given a period of credit. He must accept the bill (otherwise he will not get the goods), and accepting a bill is proof of receipt of goods in law. When the credit period is up, the bank presents the bill to the buyer once again.

Bankers' documentary credits, normally known as letters of credit, are the most expensive of the forms of payment but offer a great measure of security. The onus is on the *importer* to open a credit at his bank, in favour of the exporter. The importer's bank then informs the exporter's. The credit tells the exporter that if he presents certain documents showing that the goods have been shipped, he will be paid.

* This explanation owes a lot to articles by David Bowen and Arthur Day.

There are many different types of letters of credit. *Revocable* credits can be cancelled or amended by the importer without the exporter's approval – they are therefore very risky for the exporter. *Irrevocable* credits, despite their name, can be altered, but only with the approval of both parties. *Confirmed irrevocable* credits are guaranteed by the exporter's bank, in return for a fee – as long as the exporter has kept to his side of the bargain, the bank will ensure that he is paid. If the importer fails to pay, it is the bank's job to pursue the debt. These credits are the normal method of payment for goods shipped to risky countries. *Revolving* credits allow two parties to have a long-term relationship without constantly renewing the trade documentation. *Transferable* credits are used to allow goods to be passed through middlemen to give security to all three parties – exporter, middle-man and importer. With all these payment instruments, the finance comes, in effect, from the exporter or his over-draft. If he has to wait for, say, sixty days before being paid, he is, in effect, making an interest-free loan to his customer. Only when the credit is medium-term (more than six months) will the customer normally be expected to pay interest.

There are three further methods of trade finance which involve the exporter in passing to another institution part or all of the responsibility for collecting its debts. One is to use an export credit agency in return for a premium (see Chapter 11). The other two are factoring and forfaiting.

A company which is involved with all the problems of designing, producing and selling a range of products may feel that it has enough to do without the extra burden of chasing its customers to settle their debts. Instead, it can call on the services of a factor. Factors provide both a credit collection service and a short-term loan facility. Their charges therefore have two elements, the cost of administration and the charge for the provision of finance. Most factoring covers domestic trade but it has a distinct role in exporting.

Companies which have called on the services of a factor will invoice their clients in the normal way but give the factoring company a copy of all invoices. The factors will then administer the company's sales ledger, in return for a percentage of the turnover. They will despatch statements and reminder letters to customers and initiate legal actions for the recovery of bad debts. In addition, some companies will provide 100 per cent insurance protection against bad debts on approved sales.

Factoring is a particularly important service for expanding companies which have not yet developed their own full accounts operations. Factors will also provide short-term finance to corporations short of cash. When the company makes out its invoices, it can arrange to receive the bulk of the payments in advance from the factor. Effectively, the factor is making the company a loan backed by the security of a company's invoices. In return, the factor will discount the invoices paying, say, only 90 per cent to the company. The extra 10 per cent covers both the factor's risk that the invoices will not be paid and the effective interest rate on the 'loan'.

Like factoring, forfaiting is a method of speeding up a company's cash flow by using its export receivables. Forfaiting gives exporters the ability to grant their buyers credit periods while receiving cash payments themselves. While factoring can be used for goods sold on short-term credit, such as consumer products or spare parts, forfaiting is designed to help companies selling capital equipment such as machinery on credit periods of between two and five years.

Suppose that a UK company has sold goods to a foreign buyer and has granted that buyer a credit period. A forfaiting company will discount an exporter's bills, with the amount of discount depending on the period of credit needed and the risk involved to the forfaiting company. In order for the company to make the bills more acceptable to the forfaiting company, it will ask the buyer of the goods to arrange for the bills to carry a guarantee, known as an *aval*, from a well-known bank. The more respected the bank involved – and the less risky the country it is based in – the cheaper the cost of forfaiting. Unlike factoring companies, forfaiters often sell on these bills to other financial institutions. Their ability to do so helps reduce the cost of the service. (In general, the more liquid the asset, the lower the return.)

The main use of forfaiting in the past has been made by companies seeking to finance medium-term trade commitments (three to five years). In the past few years, forfaiting has been increasingly used as a means of financing short-term payments of three to six months.

This chapter has discussed the needs of the major borrowers in the UK economy. In the next chapter we will look at those individuals and institutions with funds to invest.

8   Investment Institutions

Nowadays the majority of the nation's shares are held not by wealthy individuals but by institutions – pension funds, life assurance companies, unit and investment trusts. They are also the biggest holders of gilts and wield significant power in the property market. The investment institutions are now among the barons of the land.

Such is the influence of the institutions that one of the reasons why the City was forced into the 'Big Bang' was in order to meet their needs. The abolition of fixed-minimum commissions dramatically brought down the costs of share-dealing to the big investors. Previously they had shown signs of being enticed away from the Stock Exchange and into the telephone-based, over-the-counter markets made by the big securities firms.

Most fund managers do not feel very powerful, however. Each of the investment institutions has outside forces to which it is beholden. Pension-fund managers must look to the trustees of the companies whose funds they administer, life assurance and insurance companies to their shareholders and policyholders and unit and investment trusts to their unit- and shareholders respectively. Conspiracy theorists can follow the chain of ownership back and back without finding a sinister, top-hatted capitalist at the end of it.

In theory, investment institutions could combine and could start altering the policies of the companies in which they have substantial holdings. However, the reality is that they rarely exercise their power to intervene in the day-to-day running of firms. That does not mean that managers can ignore their wishes: if institutions dislike a company's policies, they will sell their shares, bringing down the price in the process.

Too low a share price will attract predatory rivals, who will buy up the company, and the management will lose its cherished independence.

The time when institutional investors are most powerful is during takeovers, when both sides vie for the institutions' favours. The sizeable holdings of the institutions mean that the way they jump will decide the success or failure of the bid. In recent years the institutions have shown little tendency to be loyal to existing managements and appear to be more than willing to sell out to the highest bidder. This has brought them much criticism for their apparently short-term horizons.

THE GROWTH OF THE INSTITUTIONS

The extraordinary growth of investment institutions is due in part to the increased wealth and longevity of the population. In the past, few people survived into old age, and those who did often had independent means. As people have lived longer there has been a greater need for pensions. Few people have been satisfied with the pension provided by the state, so occupational pension schemes have evolved, with both employees and employers making tax-free contributions.

Occupational schemes come in two kinds. Defined benefit schemes contract to pay employees a set sum based on their final salary. The employer is responsible for making up any shortfall in the fund; there is rather more debate about who is entitled to any surplus. In a defined contribution scheme, the employee and employer put in monthly payments but the pension is entirely dependent on the investment performance of the fund. In short, in a defined benefit scheme, the employer takes the risk; in a defined contribution scheme, the employee takes the risk.

Each pension fund is run by a trust, which can either manage the funds itself or appoint outside fund managers. The outsiders can be banks, brokers or specialist fund-management companies. The pension-fund trustees often split up the fund between several managers to ensure that a bad set of decisions by one manager does not affect the solvency of the whole fund.

The wealth of the country has also allowed savings to be more widely distributed than ever before. In late Victorian times the population was divided into a few people with a lot of savings and the mass who had no savings at all. Seventy-five years of redistribution taxation, and a growth in the nation's wealth, mean that many more are now able to save. Until 1984 many did so through life assurance since the premiums could be offset against income tax. In recent years there has been substantial growth in personal pensions which enjoy tax exemption.

Most of the households in Britain already have some form of life assurance. The common idea of all policies is that the policyholder pays regular premiums in return for a lump sum at the end of a set period. This distinguishes *assurance* from *insurance*. An assured sum *will* be paid, and an insured sum *may* be paid, in certain circumstances (e.g. death). However, there is an element of insurance in most assurance policies, since if the policyholder dies before completing the payments, the sum will be paid immediately to his or her dependants.

The most common life policy is the endowment mortgage, whereby a mortgage is linked to a life assurance policy. When the policy matures the mortgage is repaid. These policies come in two forms: with-profits or unit-linked. The former offers a smoothed investment return; the latter a return which is more directly linked to the market.

Added to this group are the general insurance companies (see Chapter 11) which collect premiums in return for insuring property holders against risk. As the nation has grown more wealthy, people have had more property to insure. Car insurance has been a particular growth area since the war. These three sets of institutions – pension funds, life and general insurance companies – make up a distinct branch of the institutional investment family.*

They all have essentially long-term liabilities – pensions to be paid, life assurance policies to mature. They create portfolios of assets with the contributions they receive – portfolios which are designed both to be safe against loss and to provide capital growth. If the institutions invested only in one company or in one type of security, they would be exposed to the chance of heavy losses.

---

* Often life assurance and general insurance companies are one and the same thing, but there are specialized companies in each sector.

PORTFOLIO INVESTMENTS

What are the ingredients of these portfolios? A significant proportion, which varies with fashion, is invested in government securities. Government regulations require insurance companies to hold a certain number of gilts as reserves to ensure they can meet claims when they occur. Bonds tend to be more stable in price than shares.

Gilts, because of their long maturities, can be used to match long-term liabilities. Gilts also offer a high level of income and this can be extremely useful for those institutions which face a high level of payment – for example, a pension fund where most of the members are retired. The government would have enormous difficulty in funding itself without the gilt purchases of the institutions.

A further chunk of the funds' investments goes into property – buying land and then leasing it to industry for the building of factories, offices and shops. Property investment used to represent about one-quarter of the average portfolio; now it is no longer so fashionable. The boom-and-bust cycles of the early 1970s and late 1980s has perhaps discouraged some institutions from venturing into the property field. Nevertheless, property has a tradition of being a safe, long-term investment and of more than keeping pace with inflation. Perhaps this is because of the tax advantages which used to be given to the private housing market, which enable demand for private housing to outstrip supply. The rising prices for private and new houses, encouraged by the tax system, force prices up in the rest of the market.

The biggest proportion of institutional investment goes into equities, and in the next chapter we examine the effect of institutional investors on the share market. Equities have historically offered much better returns than bonds or money market instruments and thus have greatly benefited the institutions. Insurance companies, for example, often make a loss on their underwriting business but make up for this with investment profits; the gains earned by pension funds in the equity market have allowed the companies that sponsor them to reduce their payments into the fund.

The spare cash of the investment institutions goes into the money markets. Although their immediate outgoings are usually met by the premiums and contributions, the institutions still need liquid funds to meet any disparities. So they invest in bank CDs, commercial bills issued by major companies and wholesale deposits from the banks and discount houses. At certain times, when the yield curve is inverted, and when shares seem unsafe investments, the proportion invested in the money markets increases.

OVERSEAS INVESTMENTS

Not all this institutional investment takes place in the UK. In 1979, the government abolished exchange controls. This allowed the institutions to invest substantial sums abroad. In 1979, the proportion of pension fund portfolios held in the form of overseas equities was 6 per cent; by 2000, it was 23 per cent.

The amount of money that pension funds invest depends on a variety of factors. First of all, the fund managers must decide whether overseas markets look more attractive than the UK, perhaps because the prospects for economic growth and corporate profits look better, perhaps because overseas shares look better value, relative to company profits and assets.

Secondly, the managers must decide whether sterling is set to rise or fall. If the pound rises, then the value of overseas assets, when translated back into sterling, will reduce; if the pound falls, then the value of such assets may rise.

Thirdly, managers must pay attention to matching their assets and liabilities. The beneficiaries of the funds (future pensioners) will use the money they receive to buy goods and services in the UK, so it makes sense for the fund to have a large UK element. Many UK companies already receive a large proportion of their income from abroad, so investors can get a reasonable amount of diversification without leaving the London stock market.

The overseas diversification of funds used to come under some criticism from the left but with the increasingly free flow of international capital, the complaints have died down. There is little evidence that UK companies are short of capital and US and European investors are active in the UK market.

The next main set of institutional investors are the trusts. They are divided into unit and investment trusts, but both serve roughly the same function – to channel the funds of small investors into the equity markets.

INVESTMENT TRUSTS

An investment trust is a public company like any other company except that its assets are not buildings and machinery but investments in other companies. Investors buy shares in the trusts and rely on the expertise of the fund managers to earn a good return on their investments.

The origins of the investment trust movement lie in Scotland. Many of the entrepreneurs who made money out of the Industrial Revolution found themselves with surplus funds which could find few profitable homes in their locality. So they looked for advice to help them invest elsewhere and turned to their professional advisers – the lawyers and accountants. A few smart people from both professions realized that they could pool the funds of their clients and invest larger sums. That early development was complemented by the growth of Scottish life assurance companies and pension-fund managers, and today Edinburgh is still a very significant force in international fund management.

Nowadays all investment trusts must be approved by the Inland Revenue. They raise money through preference shares and loan stock as well as through equity. By late 2001, there were almost 500 trusts with over £63bn in assets.

There are a few restrictions on the way in which trusts can invest. No single holding can constitute more than 15 per cent of their investments. Capital gains must be reinvested in the business and not distributed to shareholders.

Those restrictions aside, the trusts appear in a wide variety of forms. Some, including the largest, 3i, invest across the world; others confine themselves to a single country, such as Brazil, or a specific sector of the market, such as property or mining.

The structure of trusts also gives them enormous flexibility. For example, they can borrow money to finance their investments, and the interest on their borrowings can be offset against tax. This is known as *gearing* and relies on the rate of return on the trusts' investments exceeding the cost of borrowing. If it does, the trusts' profitability increases substantially; if it does not, losses multiply.

Split capital trusts use a different approach. Most trusts offer investors a mixture of income and capital gains. A split capital trust separates the two. All the revenue of the trust is paid as dividends to the income shareholders; however, they will usually receive no capital gain and, in some cases, can expect a capital loss. The capital growth of the trust is then parcelled among other classes of share; either in a safe and steady form (zero dividend preference shares); or in a more high risk/high reward form (capital shares).

In mid 2001, some split capital trusts ran into difficulty. They had borrowed money to invest in shares, but the decline in the stock market had slashed their ability to repay. Worse still, it emerged that there were a lot of cross-holdings between trusts, so that the problems of one fund were quickly communicated to others. The losses incurred by some investors are likely to dent the popularity of split capital trusts for a while.

One of the problems of investment trusts is that their shares tend to stand at a discount to the net asset value. This means that the total value of their share capital is less than the value of the investments they hold. The discount is a function of supply and demand. There are normally not enough investors wanting to buy the shares to keep them trading at asset value. This discount varies from trust to trust, depending on the nature of the trust's investments and the reputation of the manager.

Investment trusts have grown in popularity over the last 20 years. Many have introduced savings schemes, which allow investors to buy shares for as little as £20 a month, for a very low cost. Personal equity plans, which allow investors to hold trust shares tax-free, also helped. These two factors helped discounts across the sector to narrow in the late 1980s and early 1990s.

UNIT TRUSTS

Like investment trusts, unit trusts bundle together the assets of small investors in order to give them a less risky opportunity to invest in the equity markets. Rather than buy shares in a company, investors buy units whose prices rise and fall with the value of the assets held by the trust. The unit trust managers earn their money through the spread between the buy and sell prices of the units and through a management charge.

Unit trusts have been one of the investment successes since the war. New trusts are being launched all the time, with even Marks & Spencer getting into the act in October 1988. By late 2001, around £223bn was invested in unit trusts, spread across 1,760 different funds. Although the vast majority of unit trust money is invested in equities, there is a growing number of bond and money market (cash) funds.

There must actually be a trust, whose trustees are normally either banks or insurance companies. The trustees' job is to ensure that the fund is run properly and not to supervise its investment policy. The latter task is organized by specialist managers who often are also supervising the funds of insurance companies or merchant banks.

Since unit trusts are not quoted companies, they do not suffer from the discount problem of investment trusts. Nor can they borrow money to invest. This makes them less risky than investment trusts. On the other hand, their charges tend to be higher with a 5 per cent initial charge and a 1–1.5 per cent annual charge quite common.

A new form of unit trust, called the open-ended investment company (OEIC), is gradually being introduced. These are designed to be easier to understand since, instead of separate bid and offer prices, investors buy and sell at the same price. This does not make things any cheaper for the investor, since the initial charge is added separately.

HEDGE FUNDS

A new type of investor has been making headlines in recent years – the hedge fund. When the markets move suddenly or unexpectedly, hedge funds are often cited as the culprit.

There is a lot of confusion about what hedge funds actually do – and this is not surprising. While they share some common characteristics, hedge funds appear in a multitude of guises, making it difficult to produce sweeping definitions.

The simplest definition of a hedge fund is a private investment vehicle with a limited number of very wealthy investors. But that is like defining a cat by saying it has four legs.

The reason for the name 'hedge fund' comes from the idea of hedging your bets. Original hedge funds went both long and short of the market, that is they both bought shares and sold others which they expected to fall in value (in the hope of buying them back at a lower price).

Take the two oil companies; BP and Shell. Suppose you think that BP is undervalued relative to its rival. You could buy BP shares and go short of Shell. Provided your analysis was correct and BP subsequently outperformed Shell, you would make money regardless of the way the overall market moved.

Some hedge funds still operate in that way. Indeed, Long-Term Capital Management, the US hedge fund whose near collapse prompted a financial crisis in mid 1998, followed a similar strategy; buying corporate bonds and going short of government debt.

The problems of LTCM were heightened by a characteristic of some (but not all) hedge funds – the ability to borrow. Investment trusts can also used borrowed money but not on the same scale; some hedge funds borrow many times the value of their capital. That ability allowed George Soros, the most famous hedge fund manager, to mount his $10bn attack on the pound in 1992.

Soros is the prime example of the macro hedge fund manager, those who make big bets for or against individual currencies and markets. These managers have come under attack, particularly in Asian countries, for their destabilizing effect on global markets.

But macro funds are only a small part of the hedge fund world. Most hedge funds concentrate on trying to make profits out of pricing anomalies in the market, in fields such as mergers and acquisitions of corporate bankruptcy. Their managers have no desire to be as famous as George Soros; the less publicity the better, as far as they are concerned.

UNDERWRITING

The investment institutions do more than just invest in existing shares. They also play a part in the new issues and the rights issues markets by underwriting. In return for a fee, they guarantee to buy shares at a set price if no one else will. The fees can be substantial. When Abbey Life went public in June 1985 the value of the shares it issued was £243 million. Total underwriting fees were £3 million. The underwriters had guaranteed to buy shares at the offer price of £1.80. When shares actually started trading the price jumped immediately to £2.35. The issue was a resounding success, and the underwriters pocketed their fees.

It is rather unfair to say that underwriters earn money for doing nothing. They act in the same way as insurers. Claims occur when the underwriters have to buy up shares at the offer price, and in those circumstances the loss can be considerable. Many institutions lost substantial amounts of money when BP's issue flopped in 1987 and the government had to set up a 'safety net' to help them out. For the underwriters the knack is to ensure that the sums earned from successful deals outweigh the costs of supporting failures. If underwriters tried to avoid the bad deals, the brokers who put the business their way would cut them out of the likely successes.

The BP deal indicated that, at times, underwriters can be exposed to risks. But in the 1990s, there emerged a feeling that underwriters were paid too much and that companies were incurring excessive costs in raising new capital. The Monopolies Commission investigated the subject and this acted as a spur to voluntary reform. Tendering, where investors make competitive bids to underwrite issues, was one way forward.

As we have seen, investment institutions tend to invest a large proportion of their funds in equities. The next chapter looks at the market for shares.

9   Shares

It is easy to get confused by financial jargon, and the stock market is no exception. Although people use the terms 'stocks and shares' as synonyms, there used to be a distinction, with stocks referring only to fixed interest instruments.

Shares are quite distinct from loans and bonds. Whereas someone who lends money to a company or buys its bonds is a creditor of a company, a shareholder is the owner of the company. A share, or equity, represents a share in the assets and profits that the company produces.

Unlike loans or bonds, a shareholder is unlikely ever to be repaid by the company itself. If a shareholder wants to realize his money, he must sell the shares in the open market. Furthermore, the return available to lenders or bondholders is normally fixed in advance; the return to shareholders is infinitely variable. Once a business's costs (including interest payments) have been met, all the excess belongs to the shareholders. However, if the business goes bust, the shareholders are at the back of the queue for repayment.

Shares and shareholders are unique to the capitalist system. Under a communist system, bonds are issued but never shares, since ownership of virtually all commerce is in the hands of the State. It is not exaggerating the case, therefore, to say that shares are at the heart of capitalism. They have traditionally been the investment most likely to get people rich quickly and also to reduce them to poverty (remember the Great Crash of 1929).

OWNERSHIP AND CONTROL

Shares also provide the means through which ownership of industry can be divorced from control. Death and taxes have gradually weakened the grip of the founders of old family-run businesses. Few individuals now have the capital to finance a firm's expansion. Modern industrial giants are run by boards of directors, who in turn appoint salaried managers to administer the day-to-day business of the company. Some managers sit on the board and some have shares of their own but, except in a few special cases, managers rarely own a significant proportion of the company's equity.

An attempt has been made in the last 15 years to reverse this trend by giving managers share options, which allow them to buy shares at a set price. The theory is that this will ensure that the interests of investors and managers are aligned, since both will benefit from a rising share price.

In practice, the system has certainly made many managers rich. But it has been something of a one-way bet, since the stock market was rising for much of the 1980s and 1990s and managers were able to earn huge sums just for being reasonably competent.

The richest managers of all were those who took part in so-called leveraged buyouts, in which the executives, aided by some outside investors, made takeover bids for companies and removed them from the stock market. These deals would leave the managers with a big proportion of the equity but leave the company with a big burden of debt; if things went well, the managers would earn a fortune but if things went badly, the company would go bust.

THE RIGHTS OF SHAREHOLDERS

What rights do shares confer? The most common form of share is the *ordinary share*: it gives the owner the right to vote (although there are non-voting ordinary shares), the right to appoint and remove directors and, most importantly, the right to receive dividends, if and when declared. Remember that the dividend is to the shareholder what the coupon is to the bondholder (i.e. an opportunity to receive income rather than capital appreciation).

Most companies pay a dividend every six months although some now pay out every quarter. The first appears with the half-yearly results and is known as the *interim dividend* and the end year dividend is known as the *final*.

Because shareholders stand at the end of the creditors' queue if a company fails, shares are on the riskiest end of the risk–reward scale and can therefore attract the highest return. Like bonds, shares can increase in price but the potential for share-price increases vastly exceeds that for bonds. Although dividends add to the attractiveness of shares, it is this chance of a sharp rise in price that makes shares such an exciting investment. An investor who placed £1,000 in Polly Peck shares at the start of the 1980s would have seen his sum grow to £1.28m by the end of July 1989. But a year later, the shares were effectively worthless.

Just as individual companies can go bust, the whole market can experience sharp declines. The 508 point fall in the Dow Jones Industrial Average on 19 October 1987 was only one illustration of how quickly and dramatically share prices can take a turn for the worse. It is necessary to go back only to 1974 to find a time when the FT-30 index was at 146, its lowest level for fifty years. History is littered with stock market crashes and with companies that have gone bust. The ordinary shareholders are usually the losers from such failures.

OTHER TYPES OF SHARE

In order to attract investors who are wary of the risks of ordinary share ownership, companies have devised other forms of shares which are slightly less risky. *Preference shares* are different from ordinary shares in that they give the holder a first claim on dividends and on the company's assets, if and when it is liquidated. The amount of dividend attached to a preference share is fixed. If it is not paid, it is a sign that the company is in severe financial trouble. The lesser risk attached to holding preference shares means that the return in good years is less than that of ordinary shares. In addition, the voting rights of preference shareholders are normally restricted.

Cumulative preference shares entitle the holder to be paid in arrears if the dividend is not paid one year. Since they are slightly less risky than ordinary preference shares, the yield on cumulative preference shares is marginally lower. *Redeemable preference shares* will be repaid at a future date; they closely resemble bonds and must offer a similar return to be attractive to investors. *Participating preference shares* offer a lower basic rate of return but allow for a bonus rate if the ordinary dividend is high. *Convertible preference shares* can be converted into ordinary shares at a certain price – they closely resemble convertible bonds (see Chapter 10). Again, the investor is compensated for the lower initial rate of return by the chance of future gains.

As a group, preference shares resemble fixed-rate bonds; indeed, the yield from such shares tends to be compared by investors with the yield on long-dated gilts. However, unlike bonds, companies which issue preference shares cannot offset the dividend against tax. This made them increasingly unpopular in the bull market when it was cheaper to issue ordinary shares to a seemingly insatiable investing public.

There are occasions when preference share issues are still the best option (e.g. when the existing management group is concerned that a conventional rights issue will weaken its control of the company).* By issuing preference shares as a bonus to existing shareholders and selling their own allotment to outside investors in return for cash the management can raise money without threatening its control of the company.

Companies can also issue stocks called *debentures*, which are essentially long-term (over 15 years) bonds. Debentures have advantages both to the companies which issue them and to the investors who buy them. Companies can deduct the interest payments from profits before taxation and may retain the option of early repayment. The investor has the advantage of a high level of security, since most debentures are secured by a charge on the assets of the company. In addition, debenture holders can appoint a receiver if the firm is in financial trouble and they rank above all other loan creditors and shareholders when a failed company's assets are being redistributed. Companies are obliged in law to pay interest on, and repay the capital of, debentures, regardless of whether the firm is making a profit or a loss.

* Those who are familiar with the Westland saga will know that the proposal for the minority Sikorsky-Fiat holding was to be achieved by an issue of preference shares.

TRADED OPTIONS

Traded options differ from other types of equity investment because they are not issued by the companies concerned. Instead, they are instruments traded on stock exchanges designed to give investors greater leverage and to act as hedging vehicles for those investors worried about future share-price movements.

Options grant the buyer the right to buy (a *call* option) or to sell (a *put* option) a set number of shares at a fixed price. The option buyer is not obliged to buy or sell at that price if it is not advantageous to do so. In return for granting the option, the option seller receives a non-returnable premium.

An example will help explain the principles involved.* Suppose an investor has bought British Telecom (BT) shares at £1.50. Their price moves to £1.70 each. The investor wants to make sure that he retains some of his gain, but does not want to miss out on the chance of seeing the price rise still further. So he buys a put option at £1.70 – giving him the right to sell his shares at £1.70 if he so wishes. In return, he pays a premium of five pence a share. If the share price falls to £1.50, the investor exercises the option and sells the shares at £1.70. Taking away the cost of the premium, he has retained a profit of fifteen pence. If the share price rises to £2.00 the investor simply lets the option lapse. He has paid five pence a share but has a profit of forty-five pence a share over his original purchase.

More speculative investors may try to use options for their leverage potential. Suppose an investor has no shares in British Telecom at all but merely believes their price will rise. In the above situation (BT shares at £1.70), he could buy a £1.70 call option for a premium of five pence a share (on 100 shares, that would cost him £5). If the price rises to £2.00, then the option will be worth at least thirty pence on the traded market, because he could buy his shares at £1.70 through the option and then sell them at £2.00 at the Stock Exchange. Rather than exercise his option, the investor would sell the option and receive £30, or a 500 per cent profit on his original investment. An ordinary shareholder, buying at £1.70 and selling at £2.00, would have made a profit of only 17.65 per cent.

* Examples of two other sorts of option, based on interest rates and currencies, are given in Chapter 12 and Chapter 13 respectively.

NEW ISSUES

New issues are one of the most exciting parts of the stock market. Not only do they allow investors to spot the successes of the future at a relatively early stage, they are also a direct means of providing capital for industry. Obviously, the daily buying and selling of shares – known as the secondary market – is extremely important. Without the knowledge that their shares could easily be sold, investors would not subscribe for new issues. But it is new issues – and the subsequent capital-raising exercises for expansions and acquisitions – which provide the main economic argument for the Stock Exchange's existence.

Since the Financial Services Act was implemented in 1988, there is no real forum for trading shares outside the Stock Exchange. However, there is at least a choice of tiers for companies wishing to float – the main market and the Alternative Investment Market (AIM).

AIM was set up in June 1995 and like its predecessor, the unlisted securities market, was designed to attract young and growing companies. The rules for floating on AIM are much less stringent than for the main market, and depend heavily on the advisers, or sponsors, who bring the company to the market. After some early disasters, a review of sponsors led to some leaving the market.

The name of the sponsoring house may be very important in ensuring investors' confidence in the issue. The sponsor will also advise on the timing and the terms of the issue. After Black Monday in 1987, for example, several companies withdrew their issues, on advice from their banks or brokers, until the stock market was more settled. When they returned, they were able to raise less money than they had originally planned.

There are a variety of methods by which a company can join the market. If the company is particularly large – like British Telecom or Eurotunnel – it will make an *offer for sale*. This is the most expensive method of making a new issue since it requires a large amount of publicity and also the *underwriting* of the offer by institutions. Underwriters guarantee, in return for a commission, to buy shares if no one else will. When issues go well, and investors flock to buy them, it sometimes seems as if underwriting is money for old rope. But the British Petroleum issue in late 1987 illustrated that a poorly received offer can cost underwriters millions of pounds.

Once the underwriting is arranged, a company will issue a prospectus setting out in very detailed form its structure, trading record and prospects. The prospectus must appear in at least two daily newspapers. Investors are then invited to apply for shares by a certain day. On the day that applications close, the sponsor counts up all the offers and then announces whether the issue is *over-* or *under*subscribed. If oversubscribed, this means that investors have applied for more shares than there are on offer; either their applications will be scaled down or there will be a ballot, in which only a few will get shares. If the issue is undersubscribed, the underwriters will have to buy the shares at the offer price.

In a conventional offer, investors are told the share price in advance; in a *tender* offer, they pick the price themselves (although a minimum price is usually set). When all the tenders are in, the highest will be awarded shares, then the next highest and so on down until all the shares are allocated.

Tenders are unpopular with institutional investors, since they reduce the chance of an increase in price (*premium*) when the shares start trading. Private investors also are not inclined to apply for tender offers. As a result, tenders are comparatively rare and only tend to be used when an issue looks certain to be popular.

A *placing* is by far the most common, and also the most prosaic, means by which a company joins the stock market. The sponsoring bank or broker contacts key investment institutions and asks them to take some shares; individual investors are unlikely to be approached. The placing method is cheaper than an offer for sale and tends to ensure that the shares are held in the hands of a few, supportive institutions. Rule changes in the last few years have allowed companies to combine placings and offers for sale in order to gain the advantages of both methods.

The success of all these new issue methods depends on setting the right price for the shares. The higher the price, the more money flows into the company. But the sponsor will not want to set the price too high, for fear that it will fall when dealings commence. The ideal is a modest price rise on the first day. That reflects well on the company and pleases the shareholders – in the long run that will be better for the company than squeezing the last penny out of the issue price. The sponsor's problems in setting the price will be exacerbated by the presence of stock market investors called *stags*, who are eager to make a profit out of new listings when the price is set too low.

Stags are one species of the financial menagerie which commentators use to describe different types of investor. Essentially, stags are speculators who believe that a new issue has been priced too low, and who therefore attempt to purchase as many shares as possible. If they have correctly assessed that the issue is underpriced, the shares will immediately rise in value when the issue is made. The stags can then resell the shares and make a quick profit. A good example of a successful stag deal was the British Telecom issue in November 1984. The advising bank to the government, Kleinwort Benson, was particularly worried that investors might balk at such a big issue (over £4 billion). They thought it safest to err on the low side with the price. However, it quickly became obvious that the publicity surrounding the issue had been so successful that the price would rise quickly and substantially. Indeed, by May 1985 the price of BT shares had risen threefold. Despite the attempts of the government to limit the number of shares bought by any one investor, there is no doubt that some stags made a killing.

It is possible for both the advising bank or broker and the stags to overestimate the likely demand for a company's shares. If that happens, the price of the company's shares will drop below the issue price. If that happens, the stags will have to sell the shares and take the loss or hang on to them in the hope that the price will rise. As some stags will have borrowed money to purchase the shares (planning to repay the loan with the help of the profits), a failed issue can hit them particularly hard.

Stags only really emerge for offers for sale; placings and tenders give them little chance for profit. But it would be wrong to suggest that stags are unpopular with new issue sponsors. By pushing up demand for an issue, they ensure its success. The same is true of multiple applicants: people who apply for several parcels of shares or addresses. Keith Best, the Member of Parliament who was convicted of making multiple applications for British Telecom shares, was rather unfortunate. The practice had been quietly condoned for years on the reasoning that it was better to have multiple applicants than no applicants at all.

It was only the sensitive nature of a privatization issue, where profits seemed certain, that caused attention to be focused on multiple applications. Even then, it took a Labour Party researcher to discover Mr Best's offence. Later on, when it was discovered that some people had made more than one application for the phenomenally unsuccessful British

Petroleum issue, it was suggested that the offenders' best bet was to plead insanity.

RIGHTS ISSUES

A new issue normally takes place in the early years of a company's existence. As companies attempt to expand, however, they need more funds than were provided by the original sources. There are many avenues open to raise funds in the form of debt. However, as we noted in Chapter 7, too much debt makes a company unbalanced. At some point, the company will need further equity capital.

The traditional means of raising new equity is a *rights issue*. Shares are offered to existing shareholders in proportion to their holdings – a typical offer might be one share for every four owned. The shareholder may then take up the rights and pay for the new shares or sell his rights to do so to another investor.

Rights issues are a fairly expensive way of raising new money. They have to be underwritten and the shares usually have to be offered at a substantial discount to the market price. Such are the costs that some companies have tried to find alternatives to the rights offer. But the institutions have stood firm in defence of their rights. It is a general principle of UK companies' legislation that existing shareholders should have a pre-emptive right to subscribe to any new shares on offer. Without that right, the original shareholders' stake in the company would be eroded. So except for quite small issues, UK companies can still only place shares with new investors if the existing shareholders agree.

Some companies make so many acquisitions, using shares as their means of payment, that constant rights issues are out of the question. A compromise method is called a 'vendor placing with clawback'. It works like this. Company A wants to buy Company B and would rather pay in shares than in cash. But Company B's shareholders want cash rather than shares. So Company A issues shares to Company B and then immediately arranges for the shares to be placed with outside investors, thereby getting Company B its cash. To protect the rights of Company A's shareholders, they are given the entitlement to apply (to 'claw back') any or all of the placed shares.

However, for companies wanting to raise large amounts of equity, the rights issue is the only practicable method. Blue Arrow, the employment agency, raised £837m via a rights issue when it wanted to buy US group Manpower in 1987. That was around twice as much as the market valued the whole of Blue Arrow before it launched the bid.

When considering a rights issue, the main questions facing the company and the bank or broker advising it are when to make the issue and at what price. The shares will normally have to be offered at a discount to the market price for the company's existing shares, otherwise those shareholders who want more shares will simply buy existing ones on the market. The bigger the proportion of new shares on offer (say, one to four), the heavier the discount will have to be, in order to attract the amount of funds needed.

The company will also have to allow a grace period, usually three weeks, to allow shareholders time to decide whether or not to take up their rights. If the price of the existing shares falls too far during that period, it can ruin the prospects of the issue; the discount offered may have to be substantial in order to avoid that risk.

Timing the issue is very important – if the stock market is strong, then a company can raise a lot of money by issuing fewer new shares. However, shareholders may be unwilling to take up new shares which are highly priced. If the share market is weak and a company's share price is low, then a rights issue to raise a large amount will involve issuing a large number of shares. This can dilute the control of its shareholders.

The proportion of a company's total profits, dividends and assets held by existing shareholders is unaffected by the *price* at which new shares are issued under a rights issue or the *number* of shares issued – it is the proportion of equity raised which is important. A *one-for-four issue* will create 25 per cent more shares, in other words there will be five shares in issue for every four that existed before. If existing shareholders do not take up their rights, they will own four-fifths of the enlarged company, regardless of whether the shares were issued at 50 pence or £2 each. The important question for existing shareholders to decide is whether to exercise their rights to the issue or whether to sell them to a more willing buyer. That decision may depend on whether or not they have the cash available to pay for the new shares, whether they have an interest in controlling the company and what they see as its future prospects.

How much would their rights be worth? Assume that the company offered one million shares at £2 each and that its 4 million existing shares were trading at £2.50 (a one-for-four issue). The theoretical value of the rights can be calculated as follows:

4 million existing shares at 250 pence	£10 million
1 million new shares at 200 pence	£2 million
5 million shares in total	£12 million

Dividing the total value of the company by the number of shares, £12 million ÷ 5 million = 2.40p. Subtracting the rights issue price of £2.00 gives a theoretical price for the rights of 40 pence. In fact, this theoretical value is rarely attained exactly but it is a rough guide for investors.

BONUS ISSUES

Capitalization issues, sometimes known as *scrip* or *bonus issues*, create more shares but without a resulting cash flow to the company. Each shareholder is given extra shares in proportion to his or her current holdings. These issues are essentially accounting operations, transforming retained earnings into shareholders' capital. Sometimes, they are under-taken to reduce the price of shares since it is usually believed that high-priced shares are unpopular with individual investors.

Although the price of a company's shares should theoretically fall in proportion to the size of the capitalization issue (since the number of shares has increased while the nominal value of the company has remained constant) this does not always happen. Capitalization issues normally take place during periods of high company profits, and shareholders may be encouraged by news of such an issue to improve their view of the company's prospects and thus bid up its share price.

SHARE BUY BACKS

As well as using the stock market to raise new capital, companies can also return cash to shareholders. In the past, companies tended to hang on to spare cash, on the 'rainy day' principle. But financial theory suggests they should not do so. If companies have no profitable projects in which to invest, they should give the money back to shareholders so they can make use of it.

Under a share buy back, a company simply goes into the market and buys its own shares. Not only will this help maintain the share prices, it will enhance one measure of a company's performance called the *earnings per share*.

Provided the company is earning a decent return on its business, then profits should not be dented much by the cost of share buy back. But the number of shares in issue will fall, so the profits per shareholder, or earnings per share, will rise.

It may even pay for companies to borrow money to buy back shares since corporate finance theory shows that debt financing, which is tax-deductible, is cheaper than equity.

THE STOCK EXCHANGE

The Stock Exchange* is the traditional arena where existing securities are traded. It has long been seen as one of the symbols of both the City and the British economy. The daily fluctuations in its index are seen as reflections of the nation's economic health. Many forget the *raison d'être* of the Stock Exchange – that it provides a market-place whereby government and industry can raise the long-term funds they need.

The Exchange's origins lay in the seventeenth century, when merchants clubbed together to form joint-stock companies, like the East India Company, to conduct foreign trade. After a time, some merchants sold their holdings to others, and in the process there developed a secondary market for shares in the joint-stock companies. At first, the shares were traded in the coffee houses which were then fashionable, but in 1773 the different sites for trading were centralized for the first time. By 1801, the Stock Exchange was established in roughly its modern form.

Exchange members built up some of the country's most colourful

---

* The Stock Exchange is the title of the amalgamation of the old regional exchanges. Apart from London, the Exchange has subsidiaries in Birmingham, Manchester, Liverpool, Glasgow and Dublin.

traditions. Legend has it that if a member spotted an outsider on the Exchange floor, he would shout, 'Fourteen hundred!' (for a time, there were 1,399 members), and the offending individual would be ejected into the street, minus his trousers. Another tradition which has vanished is that of 'hammering', the term used to describe the financial failure of a member firm. The term arose because in the old days failure would be announced after an official had interrupted proceedings by hammering on a rostrum.

Times change, and the old gentlemanly agreements have given way to the age of the computer. After a few teething problems, Stock Exchange deals became processed through the Talisman system. The system operated through a special Stock Exchange company which has an account in the register of every UK company whose shares are traded on the Exchange. All purchases and sales were processed through a central account and recorded on a central computer. Ownership was automatically transferred in the computer's records between buyer and seller, and the computer then generated all the necessary paperwork. The computer also calculated the required tax payments.

However, Talisman, which was introduced in 1979, became out of date. The system still required the physical transfer of certificates and contract notes and after 'Big Bang' the paperwork got out of control. In the summer of 1987, there was a vast settlements backlog which was only really relieved by the crash, which cut dramatically the volume of shares traded.

In the late 1980s, work began on a new electronics system, Taurus. This became bogged down in embarrassing delays. Eventually, the Bank of England stepped in and a new system, CREST, was devised.

Information is also provided by computer. Company announcements are broadcast on the Topic news service; and dealers' prices, instead of being shouted out between jobbers, are shown on the SEAQ (Stock Exchange Automated Quotation) system. Both are far from perfect and face challenges from rival information providers, but they have changed the style of share trading. Movements in share prices – red for down, blue for up – can be positively hypnotic viewing, especially on a day like Black Monday, when the screen was totally crimson.

A new trading system in October 1997 was introduced for the leading companies in the FTSE 100 Index. Rather than have the market makers publish buy and sell quotes, the new system displays the orders placed in the system by investors. The system is designed to be transparent and reduce the cost of dealing for institutional investors, but in its early days it resulted in some teething problems when rogue prices were entered into the system.

THE INTERNATIONAL CHALLENGE

Shares are now traded across international boundaries. Many UK shares are owned by overseas investors and UK investors have substantial proportions of overseas shares within their portfolios. Many international companies are listed on more than one stock exchange.

The London Stock Exchange thus needs to compete with other international markets. In the future, it is possible that all shares will be traded on a global electronic exchange, which could be based anywhere in the world. At the very least, there might be just one exchange for Europe, to go alongside New York and Tokyo.

For a long time the London market was the biggest in Europe, but the others have been catching up. The LSE recognized the problem by agreeing terms for a merger with the Frankfurt Exchange in the late 1990s, but the deal fell through. Now London faces the challenge not just from Frankfurt but from Euronext, the French-led group of exchanges; Euronext agreed a deal to buy the London International Financial Futures Exchange in 2001, defeating a rival bid from the LSE. Other potential challengers include Nasdaq, the US electronic exchange and virt-X, an electronic exchange partly owned by the Swiss Stock Exchange and partly owned by the international banks.

HOW INVESTORS VALUE COMPANIES

Why do share prices move up and down? What makes some companies into poor investments and others into the equivalent of pools winners? In the end, the price of a share should be equal to the value of all future cashflows that the investors will receive, discounted to allow for the time value of money. But it is very difficult to agree on the right discount rate and even more difficult to estimate all the future cashflows. So investors have to find some short cuts.

One obvious step is to look at profits. But what is profit? It is not quite as simple as deducting a company's costs from its revenues. A charge must also be made for the gradual fall in the value of a company's fixed assets. This charge is known as *depreciation*. It is a useful concept, since it prevents accounting blips (such as a sudden drop in profits because a firm needs a new boiler). Allowances for depreciation make it easier to judge the trends in a company's profits performance.

Since tax rates can vary substantially because of the proportion of profits made overseas and because of accumulated losses in the past, it is the pre-tax profit figure which is most often chosen for analysis. If a newspaper headline talks of a company's profits being up 25 per cent, then it will be the pre-tax figure that is being referred to.

But profits cannot be the only measure of corporate performance. It is easy for companies to improve their profits by buying their competition in return for shares. Shareholders will not necessarily benefit – they could end up with 5 per cent of a company earning £20m instead of 20 per cent of a company earning £10m. So an important way of valuing a company is to look at its *earnings per share* (i.e. the base profits of a group divided by the number of shares in issue). That calculation is made after tax has been deducted.

Calculating earnings per share is one step on the road towards the comparison of different companies. The next step is to divide the share price by the earnings per share; the result is the price/earnings (P/E) ratio, perhaps the most popular way of valuing shares. It gives an immediate rough guide to the time needed for the investor's initial stake to be paid back in full. If the P/E ratio is 15, then it will take fifteen years (on current earnings) to pay back the shareholder's investment. If the P/E ratio is 2, then it should take only two years. Of course, for the P/E ratio to be a perfect guide to the payback period, the firm would have to keep its profits constant and distribute all of them in the form of dividends. Both events are extremely unlikely, but the P/E ratio is still an important measure of a group's worth.

One might assume that the lower a company's P/E ratio (and therefore the shorter the payback period), the better the shares are as an investment. This is far from being the case. Since all investors would prefer to have their stake repaid in two years rather than in fifteen, if they thought that the prospect was feasible they would flock to buy the shares of the company with the P/E ratio of 2. As a result, the price of that company's shares would rise, and so consequently would its P/E ratio. Other investors would sell the shares of companies with *high* P/E ratios and those companies would see their share price (and therefore their P/E ratio) fall.

The P/E ratio thus reflects investors' *expectations* of a company's earnings power. If the ratio is *low*, it indicates that investors expect the company's earnings to fall or stagnate. If the ratio is *high*, it normally means that investors expect the company's earnings to rise extremely quickly.

Another frequently consulted index of a company's performance is the *yield*, calculated by dividing the dividend by the prevailing share price. This calculation differs from the P/E because not all of a company's post-tax profits are paid out to shareholders. Sometimes the dividend can be a tiny fraction of the profits. The rest of the company's earnings will be retained by the company to finance its investment.

Yield figures and P/E ratios are given in the *Financial Times* every day for most of the shares traded on the Stock Exchange. An important point to note is that share prices fall just before the company issues its dividend and the shares are sold 'ex-dividend'. The person selling the shares will receive the dividend rather than the person receiving them and the fall in price will reflect the likely dividend payment. Shares become cum-dividend shortly afterwards and for a few days it is possible to choose whether to buy shares ex- or cum-dividend.

There are other valuation methods. One is to calculate the value of the company's assets and then, after deducting the value of its debts, calculate a net asset value per share. If the company's share price is lower than its net asset value per share, then, in theory, it would be possible to buy the company, sell off all the assets and make a profit.

Asset value is a quite useful valuation method for some companies but in modern industry, when many businesses are service companies with very few tangible assets, it has a limited application.

In the late 1990s, investors started to use other valuation measures to assess shares. In some cases, these were designed to overcome the problem of companies that had no profits or dividends, mainly in the Internet sector. In other cases, the aim was to produce something more sophisticated than earnings per share, a figure that can be easily manipulated.

The most popular new measure was EBITDA (earnings before interest, tax, depreciation and amortization), a figure which aimed to show the cashflow of the company.

TAKEOVERS

Although corporate profitability is very important to share prices – and a sudden move into losses or extra-high profits can have a dramatic impact on a particular share – it is the prospect of a takeover that really gets investors excited. A classic example is Rowntree, the confectionery company, which was acquired by Swiss foods group Nestlé in 1988. Before the takeover, Rowntree's share price was around £4.50; the bid eventually succeeded at £10.75.

Takeovers have been the basis for many scandals in the City, and they also can arouse much passion as the managers and the workers in the target company unite to fight off the unwanted predator. The concept is quite simple – one company buys up the majority of the share capital of another. Usually, for tax and other reasons, the predator will buy all the share capital but it is not inevitable. A simple majority gives the owner the right to take all the important decisions about a company's future. Occasionally, takeovers are dignified by the name mergers and the talk is of a partnership between equals. However, in the vast majority of cases, one party has the upper hand. Genuine mergers are quite rare.

What motivates the company making a takeover? Normally, it is the belief that it can run the target company better than the existing management. This might be because the incumbent management is particularly incompetent; it might be because combining two businesses can bring cost savings; it might be because the target company has moved into industrial sectors which it does not understand. In some cases, predators may simply believe that the shares in the target company are cheap. It may be possible, once the target has been acquired, to sell off the various parts of the company for more than the whole – a process which used to be known as 'asset-stripping'.

Most takeovers involve private companies (i.e. those not quoted on the stock market). Normally private companies are owned by one individual, or a group of individuals and the predator cannot gain control without their agreement. Why do people agree to be taken over? There are lots of potential reasons. If you own 80 per cent of a thriving private company, you are in theory wealthy but your money is locked up. Only by selling your shares can you get hold of the capital to buy your dream house, luxury yacht, or whatever. Since your shares are not quoted on the Stock Exchange, few people will want to buy them. In most instances, the only practical way to realize your cash is to agree to a takeover. Another reason for a private company agreeing to be taken over is to obtain funds for expansion. A big, publicly quoted company finds it easier to pay for a new factory or set of computers.

When a predator wants to take over a quoted company, a whole set of complex rules and customs have to be followed. The Takeover Code is voluntary but, in practice, City firms have to follow its rules if they want to keep their reputation. (Or at least, they have to avoid *being caught* breaking the rules.)

It is a general principle that all shareholders must be treated equally, and many of the rules are designed to ensure this happens. For example, it is obviously in the interests of the predator to ensure that his intentions are kept as secret as possible. As soon as news of a bid leaks out, the share price of the target company will rise substantially. Thus the greater the secrecy, the more shares the bidder can acquire at lower prices. However, the proportion of shares that a predator can acquire without revealing its stake is just 3 per cent. Once that level is reached, a buyer must reveal the amount of shares he owns and any further purchases. Otherwise, other shareholders might sell their stakes at 'artificially low' prices, only to see the price rise when the bid is announced. Another rule is that a bidder cannot buy more than 30 per cent of a company, without offering to buy the rest of the equity. Again the principle of equal treatment applies. If the rule did not exist, a bidder could buy just 50.1 per cent of the equity at a high price; the owners of the other 49.9 per cent would then miss out.

So what happens when a bid is launched? Usually, a predator will try to win the consent of the board of the target company. That board has a duty to recommend the bid, if it thinks it is in the best interest of shareholders. Sometimes, the price offered is so high or the advantages of combining the businesses are so obvious that the board will agree to the offer. In such instances, bids are nearly always successful.

It is when a bid is rejected, that the fun starts. Each side will hire one, and sometimes two, banks to advise them on tactics; each will have a public relations firm putting its case to the press. On the day the predator launches its offer, it will outline the logic of combining the two businesses and describe its offer as extremely generous. The target will come back quickly with a statement proclaiming its desire for independence and dismissing the offer as 'derisory' and 'opportunistic'.

The whole process takes up to 81 days. It is up to the predator to convince shareholders in the target company that the price offered is fair and the logic of a combination sound. If the predator is offering its own shares in exchange for those in the target, it will have to show that there is a prospect of long-term growth in its own profits.

The process is kept to a short timetable. After announcing its intention of making a bid, the predator has 21 days to send an offer document to shareholders in the target company. Then the predator has 60 days in which to win the argument; if it has failed to get the majority of shares by then, it must give up the bid.

Normally, companies are only bid for if their profits record has been disappointing. So, they are in the difficult position of arguing, 'We've been bad before, but we'll be good in the future.' Target companies will usually put some flesh on the bones of their promises with a profits forecast. They will also attack the record of their opponent. If such tactics appear to be having little success, they may be forced to call on a 'white knight' – a third company which will outbid the unwanted predator. The target company will have lost its independence but it will at least have deprived the enemy of total success.

Most shareholders wait until the last minute before deciding, in case a higher bid is put on the table. The final count can be agonizingly close – bids have been disallowed because the vital acceptances were delivered just a few minutes after the final deadline. Bids tend to be terribly acrimonious, although the kind of high-profile advertising that characterized the takeover battles of the early 1980s has been discouraged. They also are very lucrative for the banks, lawyers, accountants and public relations advisers involved. The costs of a substantial bid, successful or not, will run into millions of pounds.

It is unsurprising, in the circumstances, that banks are eager to get work as bid advisers. Some of the big commercial banks have tried to make inroads in the market by financing, as well as advising on, the bid. This can leave the banks rather exposed if things go wrong. County Nat

West underwrote the £837m rights issue which Blue Arrow used to finance its bid for Manpower in 1987; the success of the bid was swiftly followed by the stock market crash and County ended up with a £49m loss on its holding of Blue Arrow shares.

There is plenty of controversy over whether takeovers are actually good for industry. Academic studies have been written arguing that the larger businesses created are rarely more efficient than the old. Some believe that the fear of a takeover restricts the managers of companies – they tend to worry about short-term results rather than investing for the long-term good of the firm. It is certainly true that some companies are more famous for their takeovers than for actually running the businesses they own. The stock market history books are littered with the names of whizzkids who built up vast empires through a series of acquisitions, only to see the whole edifice crumble in disaster.

But it is hard to see how shareholders would ever rid themselves of incompetent managements without the prospect of a takeover. It is possible that if taking companies over was made more difficult, control of industry might be seized by less open means – boardroom coups, for example. At least, under the current system, the arguments are made public.

TAKEOVERS AND FRAUD

Since so many of the City's scandals are tied up with takeover battles, it is worth explaining the practices that incur such disgust. The first is *insider dealing*. This is not an offence confined to takeovers, although bids offer most of the best opportunities. All it involves is someone – the chairman's brother, the stockbroker, the lawyer – buying or selling shares in advance of some piece of important corporate news. Say that Acme Inc. is about to bid for Dullsville. Acme employs the First National Bank of Wigan as its adviser. A young broker at the First National learns of the bid and buys a large slug of Dullsville shares just before the bid is announced. He makes a substantial profit *but* he is an insider dealer.

Not everyone thinks that insider dealing is wrong. Some think that it makes the markets more efficient, since it is a way of ensuring that all the information about a company is in its share price. It is, such people say, a victimless crime. And insider dealing is very hard to define as an offence.

There have been some scandals which involved people learning of the shares that newspapers were about to tip in their columns and then buying accordingly. But you could argue that the only people to suffer were those foolish enough to buy on the back of a newspaper tip. Then there is the question of how you obtain the information. Supposing you overhear two men in a bar saying that they think ICI is about to be taken over. The chances are very high that the two men do not know what they are talking about. If you buy ICI shares, you may actually lose money. But if, by chance, the men were right, does that make you a criminal?

The second sort of scandal involves the tactics used in the bid. Since many offers are made using the shares of the predator company as consideration for those in the target company, it is obvious that the higher the price of the predator's shares, the better the chances of the bid. Thus, there is an incentive for the predator to try to manipulate its share price, perhaps by bribing others to buy its shares. Such schemes are now against the law, but they can be difficult to prove. Similarly, if a few shareholders have large stakes in the target company, the predator may try to bribe them to accept its offer, perhaps in return for some commercial deal after the bid is successful. Again such arrangements can be difficult to prove.

THE FTSE INDEX

Every day, on the television news, some reference will be made to the performance of the FTSE Index – the so-called barometer of industry's health. If the FTSE Index goes up, that in itself is regarded as 'good' news. If it goes down and keeps falling, talk of a national crisis begins.

There are several indices in use, but the one most commonly referred to is the FTSE 100, which stands for the Financial Times-Stock Exchange 100 Index. The hundred firms involved are some of the biggest in the country – the so-called 'blue chips'.

The idea is to select companies of such size and range that they reflect both the industrial diversity of Britain and the shares involved in the market. Every time a company is taken over or falls on bad times, the index must be changed.

In earlier times, the main index that was followed was the FT-30, which as its name suggests covers just 30 companies. But that index is now felt to be too narrow a base since a large move in the price of just one firm can affect the whole index. An even wider index than the FTSE 100 is the FTSE All-Share Index. The latter, despite its name, does not include all the shares traded on the Stock Exchange but it does include all those (around 800) in which there is a significant market. Indices have also been developed to cover medium- and small-sized companies. There are equivalent indices in other markets. The US uses the Dow Jones Industrial Average and the S&P 500 index, Tokyo the Nikkei 225 average and Frankfurt, the DAX.

Does it really matter if the FTSE Index falls or rises? The answer is not clear-cut. Day-to-day shifts are of little importance. They may result from a chance remark of a government minister, from an opinion poll showing one or other party to be ahead, from an unexpected set of economic statistics or because investors expect any or all of these things to be good or bad. What actually happens to the economy or to the government is usually not as important as the *expectations* of investors about what might happen.

Remember that the vast majority of shares are held by investing institutions. They must not only judge the prospects of individual companies but also the prospects of the share market as a whole. If they think that, say, interest rates are about to fall, they might shift their portfolios into bond investments because the prices of bonds will rise as rates fall. However, they might feel that a drop in rates will reduce the costs of industrial companies and cause share prices to rise. Either line of reasoning would have logic behind it. The net result will be that some investors will sell shares and some will buy, moving the index up or down depending on where the balance lies. Such day-to-day shifts have little effect on the performance of business, although they may be costly for shareholders who buy or sell at the wrong time. Obviously a disastrous day like 19 October 1987 ('Black Monday'), when the Dow Jones Industrial Average fell 508 points, has an enormous impact. But such earth-shattering days are fortunately few in number. It is long-term shifts in the index which are important.

There is little doubt, for example, that the Wall Street Crash of 1929 contributed to the depths of the 1930s depression. In the UK, share prices bounced back in the late 1970s from their lows of January 1975 as the economy recovered from the three-day week, the miners' strike and hyper-inflation. Some thought at the time that Black Monday signalled a repeat of the 1930s. Although the 1990s recession was bad, it did not plumb the depths of that earlier era.

Through the auspices of the London Financial Futures Exchange (see Chapter 12), it is possible to buy futures based on the FTSE 100 index. If the index rises, the price of the future will also rise. Under the system through which futures are traded, a rise in the futures price benefits futures buyers and a fall benefits the sellers. That allows institutional investors to sell futures to protect their shareholdings against a general fall in prices by selling index futures. For those who do not fancy the intricacies of the futures market, several bookmakers offer simple bets on whether the index will fall or rise.

Bulls are investors who believe that share prices are about to rise, and rise substantially. They may even borrow money to invest in shares, in order to get the maximum possible benefit from any increase. *Bears*, in contrast, believe that share prices are set to fall. They will try to sell now and buy back later at a lower price. They may even sell shares they do not own, a practice known as *going short*, to try to exploit the price fall. In accordance with the risk/reward rules, aggressive bulls and bears take great risks, in the hope of making their fortunes. Anyone who went bearish before the crash of 1987 could have made a lot of money from that otherwise disastrous event.

The Euromarket

The growth of the Eurocurrency market is probably the single most important development in the international financial markets since the Second World War, because it has created a market in which borrowers and lenders can borrow and invest funds, virtually untouched by the wishes of nation states.

What is a Eurocurrency? The first Eurocurrency was the Eurodollar – the simplest definition of which is a dollar held outside the United States. A Eurocurrency, by extension, is a currency held outside its country of origin. Eurocurrencies are normally held as bank deposits. So dollars deposited in Barclays Bank in London are Eurodollars; French francs held in the same bank are Euro-French francs; a sterling deposit in Paris is a Eurosterling deposit, and so on. The advent of a single European currency means that Euro-euros will be added to the list.

How did the Eurocurrency market begin? Some people believe that the market had its origin in the unwillingness of the Soviet Union to hold dollars in New York for fear that the US government might freeze its deposits at times of political tension. However, the Russians still needed dollars to be able to conduct international trade, and they began to borrow in Europe through a Russian-owned bank, Banque Commerciale pour l'Europe du Nord, whose telex code was Eurobank.

Where did the dollars that the Russians borrowed come from? From the late 1950s onwards there were plenty of dollars around outside the United States because of the current-account deficits run up by the Americans. If a country has a current-account deficit, it pays out more of its own currency than it receives in foreign currency. Dollars were therefore flowing out of the country into the hands of foreign exporters.

At the same time the US Treasury imposed Regulation Q, which set upper limits on the level of interest rates that US banks could offer to domestic and foreign investors. Those people who held dollars outside the United States and wanted to invest them found that non-US banks were able to offer more attractive rates than their US counterparts. Thus the Eurodollar market was born.

As more currencies became convertible (readily exchangeable) following the dismantling of post-war controls, the market grew. There was a range of major convertible currencies by the late 1950s. Investors were able to put their money into Eurodollar deposits in the knowledge that they would be able to convert their holdings into their domestic currencies if they wished.

A liquid market for these deposits quickly developed, and banks began to quote interest rates for dollar loans up to a year. After a short while London became the centre of the market, restoring to the City a position which it had begun to lose to New York. This was an immensely important development: the City's financial pre-eminence, formerly a concomitant of sterling's role in world trade, had been eroded by the UK's economic problems. By comparison with its rivals, London had a distinct advantage – its position in the middle of the time zones between Tokyo and New York, which allowed London-based dealers to talk to those in other centres in the course of the working day.

Those American banks which had been precluded by Regulation Q from attracting foreign investors' deposits began to set up branches in London, enabling them to compete with the European banks in the Eurodollar market. In addition to its time-zone position, London had the extra advantage of speaking the same language as the Americans, thus making it easier for bankers to live and work in Britain.

The main participants in the Eurodollar market are banks, multinational companies and institutional investors such as pension funds and insurance companies. The growth of the Eurocurrency market was undoubtedly given a boost by the end of the system of fixed exchange rates in 1971.* The sudden changes in exchange rates which subsequently occurred could wipe out the profit margins of exporters, importers and institutional investors. One way in which these groups could try to

* See Chapter 13.

protect themselves against such exchange-rate changes was to use the Eurocurrency deposit market.

Suppose a UK car exporter has received an order from a German importer. The UK company will be paid in three months' time. If the Deutschmark falls against the pound during those three months, the UK exporter will receive less money in sterling terms. It might avoid that risk by borrowing Deutschmarks for three months in the Eurocurrency deposit market and exchanging them for sterling at the prevailing exchange rate. It now has to pay interest on the Deutschmark loan but it can invest the money in a sterling account. There will therefore be a cost depending on whether UK interest rates are below or above German rates.

In three months' time the German importer pays over the Deutschmarks, and the UK company uses them to repay the loan. If, in the meantime, the Deutschmark has fallen against the pound, that will be reflected in the lower cost of repaying the loan (in sterling terms) as well as in the lower receipts of the car sales. The two effects cancel each other out whether the Deutschmark falls or rises. An importer due to pay out Deutschmarks could protect himself against a rise in the German unit by lending Deutschmarks in the Eurocurrency deposit market.

In each case there is a risk. If the Deutschmark rises, the exporter will reap the benefit if he has not used the Eurocurrency deposit market. By using the market and by effectively 'locking in' an exchange rate, the exporter foregoes the chance of a windfall currency profit.*

When Eurocurrencies are lent or borrowed in the interbank market, interest rates are quoted on a spread between the bid and offer rates. The bid rate is the rate which a bank is prepared to pay to borrow funds; the offer rate is the rate at which it is prepared to lend. The average of the offer rates, the London Interbank Offered Rate (LIBOR), is an important benchmark for other loans.† By referring to LIBOR it is possible for banks to lend money for long periods by agreeing with borrowers to reset interest rates, every six months, at a rate above (or sometimes below) LIBOR. They thus ensure that the returns from long-term lending stay close to the cost of short-term borrowing.

It is now possible to borrow Eurocurrencies for a wide range of

---

* The same effect can be achieved by using the forward market, as Chapter 13 indicates.
† Although it is now under threat from a new European benchmark, EURIBOR.

maturities. The most commonly quoted are overnight, one week, one month, two months, three months, six months, nine months and one year, but it is possible to borrow for other periods. Eurorates for the major currencies are quoted every day on the currencies and money page of the *Financial Times*. With the growth in the size and depth of the market, many billions of dollars can be moved between banks in anticipation of tiny changes in rates (the minimum movement is normally one-sixteenth of a percentage point).

In addition to the term deposits there is a short-term tradeable instrument, the Euro certificate of deposit (Euro CD). Since Euro CDs can be sold, they give the investor extra liquidity and thus carry a slightly lower interest rate than other comparable deposits. They also fluctuate in price like longer-term tradeable instruments, so they allow investors to take a gamble on short-term interest-rate movements.

The market has a great importance in the world economy, since it provides a mechanism by which funds can flow quickly between one currency and another. As the market is largely outside governmental control, it can prove a potent weapon for destabilizing a currency. It is a brave government that follows an economic policy which might alarm the Euromarkets.

SYNDICATED LOANS

The Eurocurrency deposit market described above is a short-term market. However, borrowers who need long-term finance have also been eager to tap the market. In the earliest stages the most popular means of raising long-term finance was a syndicated loan.

A syndicated loan is merely a large, long-term bank loan which a syndicate of banks club together to provide because no one bank wants to commit that much capital to any one borrower. In the Euromarket, syndicated loans carry interest rates at a margin relating to LIBOR or EURIBOR. Companies, countries or institutions with a good credit rating can sometimes borrow below LIBOR or even the London Interbank Bid Rate (LIBID), but borrowers whose financial position is not so healthy can expect to pay a considerable margin over LIBOR.

The syndicated loan market gives borrowers access to large sources of long-term funds (often the size of loans is several hundreds of millions of dollars) in a short space of time. Another advantage for borrowers is that they can borrow as much as they want up to a certain limit. The overall limit on the loan may be $100 million, but borrowers pay interest only on the amount outstanding at any time. (This compares favourably with a bond issue, interest on the full amount of which must be paid until the bond is repaid.) Syndicated loans have been particularly attractive to nation states which wish to raise large amounts of money in a single borrowing. The advantage to banks of such loans is that they can lend long-term at rates above their normal costs of funds without committing too much capital to any one borrower.

In the early 1980s the syndicated loan market was badly hit by the number of government loans which were rescheduled or deferred by the international debt crisis. The banks were faced with bad debts which cut their profits and reduced their credit ratings. Banks became unwilling to tie up their money in syndicated loans and started to lend money in more liquid forms or even to act as arrangers rather than providers of borrowings (the two processes mentioned in Chapter 1 as *securitization* and *disintermediation*).

However, corporations and supranational institutions continued to borrow in syndicated loan form and the market continued, if not quite in the lavish style of the 1970s.

THE EUROBOND MARKET

In parallel with the growth of the syndicated loan market in the 1960s and 1970s, borrowers issued long-term tradeable instruments – Eurobonds. A bond, as seen in the Introduction, is merely a piece of paper which promises, in return for an immediate loan, to pay the holder interest until the loan is repaid. Since the original purchaser can (and usually does) sell the bond, repayment will be made to whoever ends up holding the bond (the bearer) on maturity. Attached to each Eurobond are coupons which the bearer can tear off in order to claim the interest payment. Normally the maturity of the bond will be at least two years; the maximum maturity is around thirty years, although some bonds have been issued on the express condition that they will never be repaid.

The borrower can arrange to pay back the debt by setting aside a certain amount each year during the life of the bond through a sinking fund or by waiting until the end (a so-called 'bullet maturity'). Bonds can be repaid early if a borrower buys back the debt in the traded market or if it incorporates a call option at the time of the issue, allowing it to repay a certain amount of bonds each year. The effect of all these strategies is to minimize the impact of repayment on the borrower's cash flow.

There are bond markets in most parts of the world. Traditionally borrowers raised money only in their domestic bond markets. Formerly issues in foreign markets were the exception rather than the rule. As a consequence a bond issued by a foreign institution is known as a *bulldog* in the UK, a *Yankee bond* in the USA, a *samurai bond* in Japan and so on. As we saw in Chapter 4, in the sterling market the main issuer of bonds (in the form of gilts) is the government. In the Eurobond market a whole range of borrowers issue bonds, such as corporations, banks, governments and supranational institutions like the European Community.

Some companies, governments and banks have borrowing requirements which are so large that their domestic market cannot accommodate them. It is possible for them to borrow at a much better rate abroad. Domestic investors may have already bought large numbers of their bonds and no longer wish to buy the bonds of that institution unless they are guaranteed a high rate of interest. Foreign bond issues give borrowers access to other countries' investors: Eurobond issues grant access to international investors.

How did the Eurobond market develop? In 1963 the USA imposed an Interest Equalization Tax (IET) to discourage foreign borrowers from raising capital in the US market. President Kennedy was worried about continuing US current-account deficits; he considered that these were encouraged by US investment overseas. The IET was imposed, at a rate ranging from 2.75 per cent to 15 per cent, on the purchase value of foreign bonds bought by US citizens, thus making it considerably more expensive for foreign institutions to borrow money in the USA (since they had to offer higher yields to compensate investors for the tax disadvantages). Non-US borrowers were still keen to borrow dollars, however, and therefore began to look for investors outside the USA who had dollars to lend.

Although this is the subject of debate, some people regard the first Eurobond as a $15 million issue of Autostrade, the Italian motorway company. As we have seen, a Eurodollar is merely a dollar held outside the USA: a Eurobond is a bond sold outside the country of the denominating currency. The vast majority of the early Eurobond issues were denominated in dollars – a reflection of the dominant role played by the dollar in international trade.

European bankers, especially those based in London, realized that the IET had created an opportunity which they could exploit. Traditionally dollar-denominated bonds were managed by US banks, which pocketed the substantial fees involved (0.5 per cent was then standard, and on a $50 million issue that would mean $250,000). The US banks also acted as underwriters for the issues – that is, they agreed to buy any bonds which failed to be sold to outside investors. The fee for underwriting was often as much as 1 per cent. European bankers seized a portion of this lucrative business and created a London-based market to bring together international borrowers and investors.

To whom do the banks sell Eurobonds? In the markets the legend is that the typical Eurobond buyer is the Belgian dentist, the middle-class professional attempting to avoid the stringent tax laws of the Benelux countries. Indeed, an important reason for the success of the Eurobond market is the fact that bonds are denominated in bearer form, allowing the investor almost complete anonymity. Whoever presents the coupon to the bank for interest, or the bond itself for repayment, will receive payment. There is no register of owners; accordingly, they cannot be traced by regulatory authorities. As a result investors who hold bonds outside their own countries are normally able to escape tax. Anyone who enjoyed the thriller *Die Hard* will recall that the aim of Alan Rickman's group of terrorists was to rob the office building of a vast sum in bearer bonds. In fact Eurobond investors include banks, investment management firms, pension funds and insurance companies all over the world as well as wealthy individuals like the Belgian dentists.

The main currency in which Eurobonds are issued is dollars, but they have also been issued in a wide range of units, including Deutschmarks, sterling, Canadian dollars, Japanese yen and even the Kuwaiti dinar. Borrowers are not limited to issues denominated in their domestic currency. With the help of swaps (see Chapter 12), they can issue in one currency and end up with cheap funding in another, and this explains the popularity of some currencies, such as the Australian and the New Zealand dollar.

The arranging bank has a difficult task in issuing a Eurobond. It must set a yield which will be attractive to investors but will be the lowest rate possible for the borrower. At one time, the banks were paid their fees in the form of a discount to the issue price, which led to losses if the bond was mispriced. That changed from 1990 onwards, when the fixed price re-offer system started to be used. Under this system, the banks involved agree to sell the bonds at a fixed price for a set period; their fees (usually between 0.25 and 0.3 per cent) are paid quite separately.

GROWTH IN THE MARKET

The advantages of the Eurobond market – the degree to which it is unfettered by regulation and the size of the investor base – have resulted in its truly phenomenal growth since that first issue in 1963. In that year the volume of Eurobond issues was just over $100 million. In 2000, $1.43trn ($1,430bn) worth of bonds were issued. Governments often borrow billions of dollars at a time.

When very large sums are being raised, managers will sometimes arrange a global bond issue, in which the same bond is simultaneously sold in the US, European and Far Eastern markets. This technique allows the issue to reach the maximum potential market of investors.

Once a bond has been issued, it moves into the secondary market. A primary market is one in which bonds are sold for the first time; a secondary market is one in which existing bonds are traded. Traders sit in vast dealing rooms, surrounded by electronic screens displaying the current prices of bond issues, the latest moves in interest rates and the trends in the economy. They look for bond yields which have moved out of line with the rest of the market and can therefore be bought or sold for profit. They also try to anticipate whether interest rates will fall (and bond prices will rise) or rise (and bond prices will fall). If they make the right decision, they can earn their companies a lot of money; in consequence, they are some of the most highly paid men and women in the country.

London is the centre of the Eurobond market. The Americans have tried, without much success, to switch the market to New York by setting up international banking facilities, which allow banks to treat some of their New York offices as being off the US mainland. And in 1984 it was briefly feared that the abolition of the US withholding tax (a tax on the investment by US citizens in bonds issued abroad) would lead to the Eurobond market drifting across the Atlantic. The latest challenge comes from Frankfurt which may steal a march because it is the centre of the European currency zone.

And one consequence of the single currency could yet drive the Euro-bond market away from London. In 1998, European governments brought forward the idea for a withholding tax, which would deduct tax at source for bond payments. Since one key appeal of the market was the fact that payments were made gross (leaving it up to the investor whether to declare the income to the tax authorities), such a tax might drive the market to, say, Switzerland. At the time of writing, the UK government was lobbying hard against the proposal.

The location of the Eurobond market may still be London, but it is the American rather than the British banks who now have the lion's share of the business of Eurobond arranging. The early lead of the European bankers evaporated when US banks set up London-based subsidiaries to recapture their hold over the dollar bond market.

Although we have referred to the Eurobond market in the analysis above, it is a term which is becoming less and less appropriate. The capital controls and banking restrictions which spurred the start of the market have largely disappeared, and it is now more correct to refer to an *international* bond market in which international borrowers issue bonds and notes to international investors via international securities houses. Borrowers can now issue bonds in very sophisticated forms, some of which are described in the rest of this chapter.

FLOATING-RATE NOTES

Most people are aware of the concept of floating-rate debt. After all, nearly all mortgages are a form of floating-rate debt: a building society can (and does) frequently change the interest rate to be paid on the amount borrowed. The same is true for most people's savings. The interest paid to a lender is subject to change, largely at the whim of the deposit-taking institution.

Floating-rate bonds (more often called floating-rate notes or FRNs) have been a major part of the Euromarket only since 1970. One reason was that traditionally many UK borrowers, particularly companies, preferred the idea of fixed-rate debt because they could calculate their costs in advance. (Floating-rate debt was more common in the USA.) Another snag to the development of the FRN market was agreement on a benchmark around which FRNs could 'float'. Double-digit interest rates conquered the first problem; the development of the Eurocurrency deposit market provided an answer to the second.

When interest rates are high, borrowers become reluctant to borrow long-term at fixed rates because they would then find themselves saddled with a very expensive debt obligation should interest rates subsequently fall. The interest payments on an FRN, however, rise and fall with the level of rates in the market. This is particularly attractive to banks. Most of the money they invest (lend) is lent at floating rates, so borrowing through FRNs allows them to be sure of a constant relationship between the return on their investments and the cost of their funds.

Investors tend to be especially interested in buying FRNs at times when the yield curve is inverted – that is, when short-term interest rates are above long-term rates. Since the return on FRNs is linked to a short-term rate, they provide a higher income than equivalent fixed-rate bonds at such times. Booms in FRN issues have therefore taken place when high interest rates (which make borrowers want to issue FRNs) have occurred simultaneously with an inverted yield curve (which makes investors want to buy FRNs). Such conditions existed in 1970, 1974 and again in 1984–5.

The Eurocurrency deposit market established the mechanism through which interest rates on long-term securities could be linked to short-term rates (LIBOR or EURIBOR). It had already been used as a benchmark for long-term loans, and it was easy to use it as the base rate for FRNs. Typically, FRNs are linked to six-month LIBOR (the rate which banks charge other major banks for six-month loans) and are reset every six months. Most borrowers pay a margin over LIBOR that is related to their creditworthiness. The first issue was made by the Italian public utility Enel, which paid a margin of 0.75 per cent over the mean between LIBOR and LIBID, the rate which banks are prepared to pay in order to borrow.

Over the years nearly three-quarters of the borrowers who have issued FRNs have been banks. Recently, however, more and more types of institutions have issued FRNs, particularly governments and supranational bodies. As the credit ratings of banks have declined, borrowers have been able to borrow at lower and lower spreads over LIBOR, some at rates below it.

What about the secondary market in FRNs? As we saw in Chapter 2, the level of interest rates has a major effect on the market price of fixed-rate bonds. Because they are closely linked to the prevailing level of interest rates, one might expect FRNs to stick fairly close to their issuing price. However, this does not always happen. Although the interest rate on FRNs changes, it does so only once every six months. In the intervening period the general level of interest rates can rise and fall, affecting the price of FRNs.

If interest rates rise, investors will receive a return on the FRNs which, because it is set by an out-of-date benchmark rate, is unattractive. They will sell their FRNs, causing their prices to fall, until the yields come back into line. If rates fall, FRNs will be offering a higher return than the market rate and their prices will rise. However, because the FRN rate is changed every six months, these fluctuations are nowhere near as substantial as those on fixed-rate bonds: most FRNs trade in a range of 96–104 per cent of their issuing price.

'BELLS AND WHISTLES'

Banks have developed other variations on the Eurobond, so-called 'bells and whistles', which are designed to attract investors and thereby help the issuer to achieve a lower interest rate than would be possible with a conventional issue.

One of the most prominent 'variations' is the zero-coupon bond, which, as its name suggests, pays no interest at all. Instead it is issued at a discount to its face value. Say it is issued with a face value of £100; its selling price may then be £50. When the bond matures in five years' time, the borrower will repay the full £100. The investor has effectively received all the interest in a lump, rather than spread out over the years. This can be particularly attractive to investors in countries which have tax regimes that differentiate between income and capital gains. The difference between the prices at which the bond is bought and sold is treated by some tax systems as a capital gain; capital gains taxes are normally below the highest rates of income tax. If the investor is going to pay less tax on a zero-coupon bond, he will be willing to accept an interest rate effectively rather lower than that on a straight bond. Both investor and borrower thus benefit.

It is possible to calculate the 'interest' on a zero-coupon bond, though this sounds an odd concept. Assume that the bond has a one-year maturity and a face value of £100, and that it is sold for £80. An investor who buys the bond on issue will make a £20 gain if he holds it until maturity. A profit of £20 on an investment of £80 is a return of 25 per cent per annum. If the bond had a two-year maturity, an issue price of £64 would achieve the same return (25 per cent of £64 is £16, which, added on to £64, makes £80).

Another variation is the partly paid bond. This allows investors to pay only a proportion of the bond's face when the bond is issued and to pay the rest later on. This gives them an opportunity for 'leverage'.* Suppose a bond is issued at a yield of 10 per cent and the investor is asked to pay only £50 on a bond with a face value of £100. If, because of a change in the market level of interest rates, the price of 10 per cent bonds rises from £100 to £110, then the price of the partly paid bond will rise to £60. The partly paid investor will make a gain of 20 per cent on his initial stake, whereas a conventional bond in the same conditions would have earned him only 10 per cent. Of course, had conventional bonds fallen from £100 to £90, partly paid bonds would have fallen from £50 to £40, a drop of 25 per cent as against 10 per cent (the risk/reward trade-off again).

A further potential advantage to buyers of partly paid bonds is the scope for currency speculation. Investors can buy a partly paid bond in another currency, believing that the foreign currency will fall against their own. If it does, they will have to pay less for the second part of the bond.

The problem of currency risk affects all investors who buy bonds denominated in foreign currencies. A US investor who buys an issue denominated in sterling will want sterling to appreciate against the dollar during the lifetime of the bond. Suppose the bond is worth £1 million

* As defined in the Introduction, leverage is the process of attempting to make a considerable profit from an initially small stake.

when it is bought and the exchange rate is $1 = £1. If, when the investor redeems the bond, the sterling exchange rate has risen to $2 = £1, then the investor will receive $2 million (double the original investment). However, if the pound has fallen against the dollar, the investor will receive less than his original investment.

Dual-currency bonds fix the exchange at which the investor is paid. The investor pays for the bond in one currency but will be repaid in another at a pre-arranged exchange rate. The borrower will protect this rate through the forward foreign-exchange markets (see Chapter 13).

Just as exchange-rate movements can adversely affect the investor, so can changes in the level of interest rates. Bonds have been devised to combat this risk with fixed and floating characteristics. Among the special features on offer from issuers have been the warrant and capped and collared floaters.

The warrant. This is similar in principle to an option. Warrants are normally sold separately from the original issue and give the investor the right to purchase a new bond, bearing a fixed rate of interest. The borrower gets additional and immediate cash from the sale of the warrants but incurs the risk of being forced to issue extra debt at above-market rates. The investor enjoys the prospect of profiting if interest rates fall but faces the risk that the warrants will be worthless when they expire because interest rates have stayed above the level available for the warrants.

Capped and *collared floaters.* These are FRNs where the rate can fluctuate but cannot rise above a certain level – 'the cap', – or fall below a different level – 'the collar'.

One of the problems with the bells and whistles described above is that they can be briefly fashionable, then go out of favour with the market. That can be bad news for investors who bought the bonds when they were first issued. However, one type of bond which has been a constant feature of the markets has been the equity convertible.

THE EQUITY CONVERTIBLE

Equity convertibles, as their name suggests, are bond issues which can be converted into shares of the issuing company. The company issues a (normally fixed-rate) bond. The investor may exchange each bond into a given number of shares, which becomes advantageous when the shares reach a price on the stock market which is usually 20–25 per cent above their current value. The investor has two ways of profiting from a convertible issue: through the interest rate and possible capital appreciation of the bond, and through conversion into shares, which permits him or her to earn dividends and a possible further increase in the share price. The borrower will be able to offer a reduced coupon on the original bond issue because of the potential benefits to the investor of conversion. If the investor converts, the company will increase its equity base but will dilute the value of its shares.

Another means of achieving a similar effect is to issue a bond with equity warrants attached which grant the investor the right to buy the company's shares at a set price. The difference between the two methods is that with a straight convertible the borrower gets the benefit of a reduced cost of borrowing because of the lower coupon and with a warrant the borrower receives the benefit in the form of additional cash from the sale of the warrant.

One problem with equity convertibles occurs when the share price of the issuing company falls sharply. This is bad news for bondholders, since they will be left with a low-yielding bond in a company with diminished prospects. It is also bad news for the issuer. Instead of acquiring a new bunch of shareholders on conversion, they will have to find the money to repay the bond on maturity.

This was a particular problem in the late 1980s. Companies issued convertible bonds in the bull market of 1987 when share prices were rising rapidly; after the Crash, it became clear in 1988 and 1989 that the bonds would never be converted into shares.

GETTING A EUROBOND RATING

It is almost impossible for investors around the world to be aware of the strengths and weaknesses of the multitude of borrowers who issue bonds. Largely for this reason, rating agencies have assumed an important and unusual place in the financial hierarchy. The two most famous agencies – Standard and Poor's, and Moody's – are both American. Before any bond issue, and before almost every Eurobond issue, the borrowing institution will pay one of the rating agencies to rate the issue. Standard and Poor's ratings range from AAA (the ability to repay principal is very strong indeed) to D (the bond is in default and payment of interest or repayment of principal is in arrears). Only bonds rated BBB or above are regarded as being of investment grade and eligible for bank investment.

The criteria which Standard and Poor's use for rating issue made by governments are quite interesting and give an insight into the minds of international investors. The first is political risk. The agency makes an assessment of the country's underlying political and social stability: it sees the most important factors as 'the degree of political participation, the orderliness of successions in government, the extent of governmental control and the general flexibility and responsiveness of the system'.* Standard and Poor's add: 'Signals of high political risk include such events as periodic social disorder and rioting, military coups or radical ideological shifts within the government.'

Among the social factors that the agency examines are the rate of population growth, its location and its ethnic mix. The more fast-growing, concentrated and racially diverse the population, the greater the social risk. Further factors are the degree of the country's integration into the Western political system and the extent of its participation in international organizations. The more the country is enmeshed in the Western system, so the reasoning runs, the less likely it is to repudiate its debt and therefore the better its credit rating.

An economic analysis of a country's prospects is undertaken by comparing the total of the country's debts with its foreign-exchange reserves and its balance-of-payments position. This last factor is seen by the agency as one of the most important of the economic criteria, since most debt defaults have occurred when countries have incurred persistent trade deficits. However, the standard of living of the inhabitants is also considered – the higher it is, the more able a government will be to cut down demand if it is faced with a trade deficit. A good economic growth rate also helps: the agency feels that 'A high rate of growth in total output and especially exports suggests a better ability to meet future debt obligations.'

The safest countries, and therefore those with the best credit ratings,

---

* Standard and Poor's *Credit Week*.

are the Western democracies – Third World countries and particularly those with left-wing governments are regarded as much more risky.

JUNK BONDS

Bonds are generally seen as a conservative investment. They offer more security than equities, but a lower return. For much of the 1980s, however, a US phenomenon made the bond market seem positively exciting (in financial terms, at least); this was the enthusiasm for junk bonds.

The term initially referred to bonds which had collapsed in price, normally because the company which issued them had become mired in financial difficulties. The market marked down the price of the bond because it feared the company would be unable to repay the capital, or even maintain the interest payments. In the language of the rating agencies (referred to above), the bonds would be 'below investment grade' with a rating below BBB.

A smart trader called Michael Milken, who worked for a US banking group called Drexel Burnham Lambert, saw the opportunity for profit in junk bonds. Say a bond was issued with a coupon of 10 per cent, but the company gets into difficulty and its price falls to 50 (compared with a face value of 100). If the company just pays the interest, the investor will earn a running yield of 20 per cent (10/50). And if the company repays the bond in full, the investor will double his capital.

Obviously, there is a strong chance that the company will go bust. But Milken worked out that if the investor bought a large enough portfolio of these bonds, enough of them would earn high returns to wipe out the effect of those which went wrong. His early clients who followed his advice made large amounts of money.

Later on, Milken played a key role in the takeover boom of the 1980s, financing predators with newly created 'junk bonds'. These would trade at, or near, face value, but would offer much higher yields than other bonds in the market (to reflect the higher risk). The term junk bonds extended to cover all high-yielding bonds of this type.

Milken fell from grace and was eventually jailed, and many investors who bought junk bonds at the peak of the market lost money. As with other financial theories, by attempting to exploit it so heavily, Milken and his followers altered the rules. If there was any merit to the junk bond theory, it was because few people bothered to follow the market and it was therefore possible to find bargains. Once everyone started to get interested, the bargains disappeared and investors started to forget the heavy risks involved.

LOAN FACILITIES

Companies may not want to raise money via a bond issue, on which they have to pay interest throughout its life. In the 1980s, it was quite common for companies to borrow via loan facilities, which allowed them to draw down money when they wanted it. In return, they would pay a commitment fee to a panel of banks, for agreeing to lend the money at any time.

These facilities were known by a variety of acronyms, such as RUFs and NIFS. In the late 1980s, the most common was the MOF or Multi-Option Facility which allowed the borrower to borrow money in a variety of forms, such as in different currencies or over different periods.

The 1990s recession caused so many bad debt problems that banks began to regret having committed themselves to so many facilities, often at very low spreads. Many overseas banks decided to withdraw from the UK lending market. This caused immense problems for companies trying to renegotiate their facilities; they had to deal with a large number of banks, but some of whom were unwilling lenders.

The early 1990s saw a shift to so-called 'bilateral lending', as companies decided to opt for a series of loans from individual banks, rather than group all the banks together in a complex facility.

11 Insurance

Almost everyone in the country has insurance of one form or another whether it is for their house, their car or their life. Most have insured all three and more besides. Companies need insurance as much as individuals – for damage to factory buildings or equipment and even against claims for damages from aggrieved customers. The result is a multi-million-dollar industry represented by insurance institutions which, as we saw in Chapter 8, play a vital part in the financial system and in the economy, because of their role as investors in industry.

The insurance sector has, since World War II, been one of the country's biggest foreign-exchange earners. It plays a vital role in assuming part of the risk involved in industry. Without insurance, a severe fire, for example, might render a department store bankrupt. With insurance, the company can concentrate on the *commercial* risks it faces (i.e. whether it can attract enough customers). In return for assuming an insurance risk, insurers charge a premium. They hope that their premium income will exceed the money they have to pay to those with legitimate insurance claims. If an insurance company feels that the risks it runs are too great, it can pass some of them on to a second company, the process known as *reinsurance*.

Financial institutions, by providing this service, oil the wheels of the economy just as they do by giving savers a home for their funds and by lending the proceeds to industry for investment. And providing protection against the risk of fire or theft is little different in theory from protecting against a rise in interest rates or a fall in sterling. It is just a question of calculating the risks and setting the premiums accordingly.

But the business is a highly volatile one. The UK consumer market can be highly competitive as new competitors move into the business, driving down premium rates. The last 10 years has seen the emergence of direct insurers, who sell policies over the telephone rather than via branches or door-to-door agents. These groups, such as Direct Line, have captured large portions of the market; they have also concentrated on the better risks, leaving the older companies to insure the less attractive areas of the market.

At the same time, the international market was affected in the 1990s by a series of disasters, such as Hurricane Andrew and the San Francisco earthquake, which brought heavy losses for insurance groups. Even those catastrophes pale into insignificance beside the potential losses if say, a hurricane were to hit a major US city directly.

The insurance industry has responded with a series of mergers, both in the high-risk end of reinsurance and in the consumer sector, where savings can be made in the back office. The number of UK insurers is likely to shrink significantly in coming years.

LLOYD'S

The changes in the insurance market have had a particular impact on London's most famous insurance market, Lloyd's. A series of scandals and financial problems have significantly reduced the market's importance and prompted substantial changes in the way the market operates.

Lloyd's of London developed from a coffee house opened by one Edward Lloyd just before 1687. Gentlemen from the City used to meet there and discuss insurance over their beverages. By the middle of the eighteenth century they decided that they might as well make it their main place of business.

From the beginning, the speciality of Lloyd's was marine insurance, helped by the fact that England has traditionally been a great naval power. Like underwriters in the other financial fields we have looked at (bonds and shares), Lloyd's underwriters accept a payment (in this case called a premium) in return for providing against an unfortunate eventuality. In the case of underwriters of financial instruments, they guarantee to buy the bonds if no one else will, in return for a premium. Early Lloyd's underwriters agreed to pay shipowners for the damage to, or loss of, their ships and cargo. For a long time, Lloyd's had the best intelligence on the movements of foreign shipping. Perhaps the most famous occupant of Lloyd's is the Lutine Bell, which is rung when important news is about to be announced (one ring for bad news, two rings for good).

THE LLOYD'S STRUCTURE

An elaborate structure has been built on the flimsy edifice of a coffee house. There are now six classes of individual which are involved in Lloyd's. First and foremost, there are the *clients*. Merchant shipping has long since passed its peak and Lloyd's now provides insurance for a wide variety of customers and products, including film stars' legs, potential kidnap victims and space satellites. Sometimes the clients may be other insurance companies and markets for whom Lloyd's provides reinsurance.

The second tier in the structure are the *brokers*. They link client with underwriter in return for a commission. Their business is rather less risky than the underwriters', since they are not liable to pay out for any claims. But with Lloyd's challenged by other insurance markets around the world, Lloyd's brokers have been forced to travel far and wide to drum up business. Not all of it goes to Lloyd's; indeed the bulk goes to outside insurance companies. However, Lloyd's still retains the flexibility that encourages brokers to place with it substantial or unusual risks. Brokers provide a service which goes beyond merely broking: they advise clients on the best kind of insurance protection for their needs and they act for clients by administering their insurance business and by collecting any legitimate claims they may have. The big broking firms have gradually come to dominate the market, in the process buying many underwriting agencies. As we shall see, this has led to many problems.

The next tier up are the *underwriters*, who actually take on the insurance risk in return for premiums. Many underwriters put up their own capital but it is a business only for those with strong nerves and large wallets. So great are the risks that underwriters club together in syndicates, to spread the costs among many. There are over four hundred underwriting syndicates divided into four main sections: marine, non-marine, UK motor and aviation. Even so, the combination of high taxes and safer alternatives has meant that there is a limit to the numbers of people who can become active underwriters.

To bring in the capital to allow the market to work efficiently, Lloyd's has to attract outsiders. Hence the need to bring in outside investors, names (private individuals), corporate capital and agents (to service these investors).

The *names* are wealthy individuals who club together in a syndicate to bear the risk of underwriting but allow the underwriting decisions to be made by a specialist (a working name) on the floor of Lloyd's. Being a name was standard practice for wealthy and upper class individuals for much of this century. There were tax advantages, income was steady, and disastrous years were few. That was until the mid 1980s, when losses started to pile up and many names were ruined.

The problem was the principle of unlimited liability which underpinned the market. If you invest money in Marks & Spencer and the company goes bust, you have lost your stake and that is it. Under unlimited liability, the market can come for the rest of your savings or your home in order to meet the losses.

The individuals concerned were horrified when the full extent of their losses became clear. Many claimed they had been misled about the risks; some said they had been defrauded and placed in syndicates which bore the heaviest losses. A sizeable number said they could not, or would not, pay which led to lengthy court cases and negotiations about a settlement.

The only answer for Lloyd's was to bring in new capital to strengthen the market. A series of corporate vehicles were established, which had the crucial advantage of limited liability; investors' losses were limited to the amount of their stake.

This corporate capital quickly came to dominate the market; by mid 1998, the amount of capital provided by names made up only 40 per cent of the total. The number of names, which reached 34,000 in the 1980s, dropped to below 7,000. Auctions were arranged which allowed corporate investors to purchase a name's interest in the market.

The new market structure has not eliminated the need for agents, such as *underwriting agents*, who decide whether to accept business on behalf of their syndicates. If they are a working name themselves, the agents can underwrite business on their own behalf and earn fees from using their syndicates' money to insure a proportion of the same risk.

There are also *members' agents* who act as a sort of dating agency for names: they earn a fee in return for introducing names to Lloyd's and for placing them on profitable syndicates.

In theory, underwriting can be immensely profitable. The capital employed by the underwriter can be invested so that it earns interest. (Or invested in equities. This is the secret of how Warren Buffett made his fortune. He applied his immense skill to investing the capital of an insurance company.) The premium income that results from assuming risk can also be invested; the key is that the premiums are received long before any claims have to be paid out. If premiums exceed claims, there is also a profit. An underwriter's money is thus working several times over. In addition, Lloyd's has certain tax privileges. Underwriters can carry forward losses in order to offset them against underwriting profits for tax purposes in future years.

The effect of investment earnings means that underwriters can afford to pay out slightly more in claims than they receive in premiums and still make a profit. However, if the deficit between claims and premiums becomes large, the arithmetic begins to look less healthy.

To clarify the system, let us examine a typical Lloyd's deal.* A client with an insurance risk to cover, such as a ship's cargo, will place his business with a broker. It is the broker's business to find underwriters who will cover the risk. To do so, he will go into the underwriting room.

The underwriters sit in long rows of what are called boxes (they actually consist of two benches and a desk). The broker sits down next to the underwriter and hands him a slip detailing the client's insurance need, uttering by time-honoured custom the words 'Let me broke you this,' as he does so.

The underwriter, if he accepts the risk, will set the premium and the broker's commission and then stamp the name and the number of a syndicate on the slip. His names are then committed to the deal. However, the underwriter will accept only a very small percentage of the risk and it will then be up to the broker to find other underwriters to accept the rest. If the underwriter asks questions about the nature of the risk and the client, it is up to the broker to answer as honestly as he can to ensure that the deal is made in 'utmost good faith', as the Lloyd's motto goes.

---

* This explanation owes much to Godfrey Hodgson, *Lloyd's of London: A Reputation at Risk* (Penguin, 1986).

REGULATING LLOYD'S

A series of scandals in the late 1970s cast doubt over Lloyd's ability to regulate itself and led to the passing of the Lloyd's Act in 1982. A new committee was appointed on which representatives from outside the market were introduced and a chief executive brought in from the Bank of England.

But the reforms were unsuccessful in assuaging the market's critics and self-regulation was condemned by a parliamentary committee report in 1995. Eventually, the market itself accepted that the system would have to change and in future it will be regulated by the Financial Services Authority (see Chapter 15).

Meanwhile, the shift from names to corporate capital might have helped protect the long-term future of the market but did nothing to deal with the past losses. That problem was dealt with by the creation of a new company called Equitas, which reinsured more than £8bn of the market's old liabilities. As part of this process, a settlement was reached with the loss-making names and most (but not all) of the legal cases were dropped.

Lloyd's had emerged, battered and bloodied, from a decade that had almost destroyed it.

GENERAL INSURANCE

The insurance companies that most people deal with are not members of Lloyd's. Some specialize in life assurance and some cover the whole range of policies from life to vehicle insurance. Between them, these companies represent a substantial category of the institutional investor sector, whose characteristics we examined in Chapter 8.

Most of the big companies are *proprietary* companies (i.e. owned by shareholders in the same way as a normal business). Some, however, are mutual companies which are owned by the policyholders in the same way as building societies are owned by their depositors.

There is quite a difference between life and general insurance businesses. The liabilities of life companies are much easier to assess; they can consult actuarial tables to see, on average, how many people die over a given period. They also have to make payouts to people whose policies mature, but they have plenty of leeway to reduce those payouts (by paying a smaller terminal bonus) if investment conditions are poor.

As general insurance businesses have found, their liabilities are much less predictable. Freak weather can lead to increased claims for storm damage; crime rates continue to rise rapidly; claims can be exaggerated by fraud.

THE PROBLEMS OF INSURERS

Since World War II, insurers have been faced with continuing expansion of the scale of risk. The risks of new developments like computers and space travel are very difficult to assess, since there are no track records to follow. The decline in the old heavy industries and their replacement with high technology seems, in fact, to have greatly increased insurers' risks. As one writer put it, 'Large-volume, low-unit-value, low-hazard risks have been replaced by small-volume, high-unit-value, high-hazard propositions.'* The litigious nature of US society, and the high awards paid by US courts, have created one set of problems; the gradual development of laws in areas such as pollution and product liability has added another. Insurers have faced claims out of all proportion to what they might have expected when they agreed the business.

The same pressures have applied in the reinsurance market, which has borne the brunt of heavy catastrophe-related claims. The industry has consolidated, as companies have sought the size required to pay out on large claims without facing ruin. Alternative forms of capital have been found, such as catastrophe bonds, which pay a higher rate of interest but face the risk of capital loss if claims are made.

Life companies faced their own unexpected set of risks in the 1980s, when the sudden appearance of AIDS led to the possibility that they might be overwhelmed with claims. In the event, AIDS proved less of a killer than had been feared, but the disease opened up a new area of controversy.

Companies started to ask lifestyle questions, designed to find those

* Article by W. A. P. Manser in the *Banker*, November 1985.

most at risk of AIDS, so that they could be charged higher premiums or even refused cover. While such questions have long been asked of smokers, the prospect of excluding homosexuals from cover raised much protest.

In the 1990s, the issue was broadened to cover genetic details. If insurers knew your genetic background, they would find it much easier to predict your susceptibility to certain diseases, and thus could adjust their premiums accordingly. But there are obviously huge issues of privacy involved.

Modern society could not function without insurance. The fact that individuals and companies know they are covered against disaster makes business and risk taking possible. But the industry is involved in a constant struggle to cope with changing risks and laws and with a highly cyclical business. When times are good, capital floods in and drives down premiums; when times are hard, losses on underwriting can be ruinous.

12 Risk Management

COPING WITH INTEREST-RATE RISK

A problem that faces all borrowers and investors is the possibility that future interest-rate movements will leave them at a disadvantage. A company can choose either to fix its borrowing rate or to let the rate follow the trends in the market. Each decision has its potential disadvantages. A company which borrows at a fixed rate when market rates are 20 per cent will find itself regretting the decision if rates fall to 10 per cent. Similarly, borrowing at a floating rate may ensure that the company's borrowing costs are in line with those in the market, but if rates rise during the lifetime of the loan, the borrower may regret not having fixed the rate.

In each of the above cases investors are exposed to the opposite outcome. If they have lent at a fixed rate, they hope that interest rates will fall rather than rise. If they have lent at a floating rate, their returns will always stay in line with the market. However, if rates fall, they will regret not having fixed the rate on the loan at the prevailing market levels.

Institutions which have borrowed large amounts will try to ensure that they are not over-exposed to interest-rate movements. They will accordingly aim to strike a balance between the proportion of their debt which has a fixed interest rate and the proportion which is floating. Fixed-rate funding is normally available only long-term, and UK companies have been notoriously unwilling to borrow on a long-term basis. As a result they are extremely vulnerable to interest-rate increases – a fact proved by the sharp falls in profits and the job losses throughout much of the British manufacturing industry during the early 1990s.

It is important to strike a balance between short- and long-term debt. Too much short-term debt means that the company is very vulnerable to sudden interest-rate rises; too much long-term debt means that the company may find itself with higher than average borrowing costs, both because long-term borrowing is frequently fixed-rate and because, as we saw in Chapter 2, long-term rates are often above short-term. It is also essential for companies to structure the maturity dates of their debt very carefully. If too much debt matures (and is therefore due for repayment) in any one year, the company may find itself short of funds with which to repay the debt. Companies aim, therefore, to structure their debts so that the amounts due to be repaid do not fluctuate violently from one year to the next.

The ideal debt portfolio would have a mixture of fixed- and floating-rate debt and would have as wide a range of maturities as possible. However, such ideals are hard to attain, and most companies find themselves with portfolios that are extremely vulnerable to a rise in interest rates. When that happens the financial markets offer a range of instruments as protection, including the forward-rate agreement, the financial future, the interest-rate option and the swap. They are equally useful to investors who wish to protect the value of their portfolios. Such products have been developed in the last twenty years partly because interest rates have been volatile and partly because banks have been eager to develop new fee-earning products to replace their old loan business.

FORWARD AGREEMENTS

A forward/forward, or forward agreement, is simply an arrangement between two institutions to lend or borrow a set amount at a set rate for a set period which will not begin for some months. Suppose, for example, a company knows that it wants to borrow £1 million for a six-month period commencing in six months' time. Rather than wait six months and accept whatever interest rate is then applicable, the company decides to fix the rate in advance and arranges with a bank a forward agreement.

If six-month interest rates are 10 per cent and twelve-month interest rates are 10 per cent, what rate should a bank charge for a six-month loan, beginning six months from now? Surprisingly, the answer is not 10 per cent.

Suppose the amount to be borrowed is £100. If the bank agrees to lend under a forward agreement, it will set aside that £100 for six months until the agreement begins by investing it in a six-month deposit. At the end of six months it will have accumulated £105 (£100 + £5 interest). The bank can now compare its return with the return it would have received had it invested the original deposit for a year, which would have been £110 in total. Under the forward agreement it has £105 after six months and need only charge 9.52 per cent for the second six months to achieve a total return of £110. The rate which the bank will charge for the forward agreement will therefore be slightly over 9.52 per cent (assuming that the bank has no strong view about the direction of future interest-rate movements).

Why does the bank not just avoid all the complex calculations and charge 10 per cent? One answer is competition. Other banks can make all the same calculations and offer a borrower a better rate. The second answer is in the hands of the potential customer. It could effectively create its own six-month forward rate by borrowing £100 for a year and investing the proceeds for six months. At the end of the six months it would have earned £5 interest. It could reinvest that at 10 per cent per annum for six months and earn 25 pence (assuming that interest rates have not changed in the meantime). The effect will be that it pays £10 interest on the year loan but earns £5.25, so paying £4.75 interest net, a rate of 9.5 per cent. Thus the customer need not accept a forward rate much higher than that.

The problem with forward agreements is that they involve the actual borrowing of a sum. If a borrower is seeking to cover existing debt, the effect is to double his credit lines. As a consequence, less cumbersome instruments have been developed which do not involve the principal sums.

Forward-*rate* agreements (FRAs) establish interest rates for borrowers, for lenders or for a set period in advance. When that period is due to begin the parties settle the difference between the prevailing level of interest rates and the rate agreed under the FRA.

Suppose a company has a long-term bank loan on which it pays interest at a floating rate that is reset every six months. At the start of the year the company may decide that it does not want to pay more than 10 per cent interest on the loan during the second half of the year. So the company takes out an FRA with a bank (this can, but need not, be the same bank as the one with which the company has the loan). When 1 July arrives the six-month market interest rate is 11 per cent, 1 per cent more than the company has agreed to pay under the FRA. So the bank pays the company 1 per cent to bring its borrowing costs down to 10 per cent. Had interest rates been 9 per cent on 1 July, the company would have paid the bank 1 per cent.

Unlike in the forward/forward market, no principal sum is transferred. Notional principal is agreed which matches the size of the loan so that the FRA covers the company's risk. The important part of an FRA, though, is the *rate* at which it is arranged.

FINANCIAL FUTURES

Financial futures are among the biggest growth areas in the world of finance. Their origin lies in the world's commodity markets. In the last century Chicago traders, aware of their vulnerability to sharp swings in agricultural prices, began to quote prices for the delivery of produce many months in advance. Soon trading in wheat, pork belly and coffee 'futures' (as they became known) became as vigorous as trading in the commodity itself. Precious and industrial metals, like gold, silver and copper, soon developed their own futures markets.

Trading on the futures exchanges was traditionally conducted by open outcry (the less polite term for it is 'shouting') in floor areas called *pits*. The London International Financial Futures Exchange used to be a riot of colour with each firm's traders wearing different, brightly coloured jackets. If prices are moving fast, a futures exchange can seem like Bedlam as traders desperately seek others who are ready to buy or sell contracts. (A good example of futures trading appears in the film *Trading Places*.) Outside clients can deal with floor traders only through brokers and therefore have to pay their commissions.

In the late 1990s, however, LIFFE abandoned trading in the face of competition from the German futures market. Trading moved to a screen based system, which was designed to be cheaper for investors. However,

Chicago, the world's biggest futures market, retains the pits and coloured jackets.

With the advent of floating exchange rates (see Chapter 13), it occurred to Chicago traders that there may well be a market for trading in currency futures, since exchange rates seemed to be exhibiting the same volatility as commodity prices. Currency futures quickly became a success; some experts now estimate that 10 per cent of all US foreign-exchange transactions take place on the Chicago futures floor. After the late 1970s and early 1980s had seen equally sharp moves in interest rates the Chicago traders developed interest-rate futures.

How are interest-rate futures used? Essentially, if an institution is worried about the effect of a rise or fall in the level of interest rates, it should buy or sell interest-rate futures to the extent that any movement in interest rates will be cancelled out by a change in the value of the future. The price of an interest-rate future is determined by subtracting the implied interest rate from 100. Thus a futures price of 88 would imply an interest rate of 12 per cent. When interest rates fall, the price of interest-rate futures rises. A cut in rates of 2 per cent will normally push up the price of the future by 2 points; conversely, a rise in interest rates will cause the futures price to fall.

Futures are especially useful as a mechanism for protecting against interest-rate risk because only a small proportion of the nominal value of the future (the margin) is required to be deposited. That margin is adjusted as the price of the future rises or falls. Since both sellers and buyers must deposit margin, it is possible to use futures to cover both the risk of an interest-rate rise and (if you are an investor) of an interest-rate fall.

To see precisely how a future works, suppose that a UK company knows in September that it will need to borrow £1 million for three months in the following December. The company might worry that interest rates could rise in the interim from the September level of 10 per cent. As the company fears an interest-rate rise, it sells futures (remember, a rise in rates leads to a fall in the price of futures).

On LIFFE the nominal size of the sterling interest-rate contract is £500,000. To cover its £1 million risk the company therefore sells two sterling contracts. Each contract carries a margin (set by LIFFE) of £1,500, so both buyer and seller deposit £3,000 with LIFFE's clearing house.

By November interest rates have risen to 12 per cent, the very event that the UK company feared. The futures price has duly fallen from 90 to 88.* This means that the position of the futures buyer has deteriorated, since he or she has bought for 90 something which has now fallen to 88. The position of the seller (the company) has improved. The clearing house accordingly credits the account of the seller and debits the account of the buyer. Each full point that a futures price moves is worth £1,250.† So the company's position has improved by £2,500 per contract, or £5,000 on its whole position. The futures buyer, however, is £5,000 worse off, and the clearing house accordingly asks the buyer to pay additional margin to bring his or her net position back up to £3,000.

Shortly before the contract is due to expire the buyer and seller agree to close out the futures position without actually exchanging the £1 million. (Most financial futures contracts end without the nominal contract being exchanged.) The clearing house then gives the seller the original £3,000 margin plus the £5,000 payment to reflect the improvement in the company's position. The buyer also receives back the £3,000 margin, but since he or she has paid £8,000, in all the net position is a loss of £5,000.

How has the futures transaction helped the company that was worried about the interest-rate rise? Remember that it was due to borrow £1 million for three months. Had interest rates been 10 per cent, the cost of borrowing £1m for three months would have been £25,000. However, interest rates rose to 12 per cent in November, and the company's borrowing cost became £30,000, an increase of £5,000. The profit from the futures transaction therefore met the extra cost of the borrowing exactly. The company was able to protect itself against the rise in interest rates. Had interest rates dropped, the company would have lost on its futures position but had lower borrowing costs.

The most frequent users of interest-rate futures are not companies but banks and institutional fund managers. Many company treasurers have been unwilling to accept the work needed to keep up with the margin payments involved. Banks use futures to cover their open positions when

* The futures price rarely traces the cash market this neatly. Expectations of future interest-rate movements play an important part, as do supply and demand in the futures market. However, for simplicity the example assumes a close correlation between futures and cash-price movements.

† The size of the contract is £500,000; the base price of the contract is 100; and £500,000 divided by 100 = £5,000. The contract lasts for three months; £5,000 divided by four = £1,250.

they have failed to reach their investments with their liabilities. The fund managers use futures to ensure that a fall in interest rates does not reduce the return on their investments. To do so they *buy* rather than *sell* futures. A fall in interest rates will lead to a rise in the futures price which will offset the losses on investors' portfolios.

In Chicago the vital ingredient that makes the futures market such a success is a group of speculators, affectionately known as locals. Although futures are useful for those who are concerned about existing loans or assets, they also offer a means of reaping substantial profits from a small initial position, the process known as *leverage*. As we saw in the example above, an initial deposit of £3,000 gave both buyer and seller an interest in £1 million. The company achieved a profit of £5,000 on an initial deposit of £3,000, a promising return for a three months' investment. It is this sort of opportunity for profit that the Chicago locals hope to exploit. Leverage, however, works both ways – the futures buyer in the example lost £5,000 – so locals can as easily be ruined as they can be made millionaires. However, by seeking to take advantage of these speculative opportunities, locals provide the liquidity that helps the banks, fund managers and companies to use the markets effectively.

LIFFE never had the local interest that made Chicago such a success but it was very successful after a slow start in 1982. It suffered from one weakness in that the UK markets, where it had a natural advantage, were not that interesting to international investors.

While LIFFE compensated very well for a while by dominating the business in German government bond futures, it gradually lost that market to its natural home in Frankfurt. In late 2001, LIFFE agreed to be taken over by the European exchange, Euronext.

INTEREST-RATE OPTIONS

Under the interest-rate option, which is in some ways a refinement of the forward-rate agreement, an option buyer purchases the right (but not the obligation) to lend or borrow at a guaranteed interest rate. In return the option seller receives a payment known as a *premium*, generally paid at the time the option is sold. On the day the option expires it is up to the option buyer to exercise the option and to lend or borrow at the guaranteed rate if it is possible to do so. However, if the option buyer can achieve a better rate of borrowing or lending in the money markets, he or she will let the option lapse. The maximum loss to the option buyer is therefore the cost of the premium. The size of that premium depends on three factors: the relationship between the interest rate guaranteed under the option and the interest rate in the money markets; the time left before the option is due to expire; and the option seller's assessment of whether interest rates are likely to move quickly.

If, for example, a company wanted to buy an option to *borrow* at 8 per cent at a time when interest rates were 10 per cent, there would be automatic potential for profiting from the option. As a result, the premium for the option would be at least 2 per cent and would be much larger than the premium for an option to borrow at 12 per cent in the same circumstances. An option to *lend* at, say, 12 per cent when interest rates were 10 per cent would carry a large premium, however, since it would have built-in profit potential.

Options which run for longer periods will also carry larger premiums. This is because the probability is greater that, over a long period, rates will move in such a way that the option will become more profitable to exercise. The option seller will charge a larger premium to reflect this extra risk.

How quickly interest rates will move is the hardest of the three elements for the option seller to assess. If the rate has shown a tendency to fluctuate violently in the past, it will obviously carry a higher premium than a rate which has shown a tendency to be stable.

An example will help to clarify the point. A company buys a three-month option to borrow at 10 per cent for three months, based on a nominal principal sum of £1 million. At the time the option is sold, interest rates are 10 per cent and the option seller charges a premium of 1 per cent (£2,500).

Outcome 1   At the end of the three-month period interest rates are 12 per cent. The company exercises the option, thus borrowing at a rate 2 per cent cheaper than if it had not bought the option (this is equivalent to a saving of £5,000). However, the premium cost 1 per cent (2,500), and the savings that the company makes (compared with its borrowing costs if it had not bought the option) are £2,500.

Outcome 2   At the end of the three-month period interest rates are

8 per cent. The company lets the option lapse but is free to borrow at the cheaper rate available. Its extra costs are £2,500, the cost of the premium, but its borrowing costs are £5,000 less than it might have expected at the time when it bought the option.

SWAPS

Swaps were once seen as exclusive products which were tailor-made to suit the few sophisticated borrowers who could understand them. Nowadays they are a huge global market, with many simple, standardized products.

The basic concept behind the interest-rate swap is that two borrowers raise money separately and then agree to service each other's interest payments. However, many swap deals are much more complicated and can involve several currencies and half a dozen borrowers, with only the bank in the middle aware of all the details.

Why should two borrowers want to pay each other's interest? There are two main reasons. The first concerns the different perceptions of different markets. Investors in one country may be prepared to lend to a US borrower at an advantageous rate but will ask for a higher rate from a UK borrower. In another country it may be the UK borrower who receives the better rate. In those circumstances it can benefit both borrowers to raise funds in the market where their credit is best and then swap the funds.

An example of an early swap deal may help to explain. The World Bank and IBM both wanted to raise funds, the World Bank in Swiss francs and IBM in dollars. Swiss investors had already accepted a good deal of World Bank debt and would accept more only if it were offered at a higher rate. They were keen, however, to invest in a top US corporation like IBM. In the USA the World Bank's credit was perceived as being better than IBM's. So the World Bank borrowed in dollars and IBM in Swiss francs. They then arranged a swap, so that IBM got its dollars and the World Bank its Swiss francs. Each ended up paying less than if they had borrowed separately. Such are the opportunities for borrowing at advantageous rates through swaps that in some years 80 per cent of Eurobond issues have been swap-linked.

The second reason for arranging swaps concerns the different perceptions of *borrowers* as to the likely direction of future interest-rate movements. As we have seen, borrowers can choose to borrow either at a fixed or at a floating rate. If they think interest rates will rise, they should borrow fixed; if they think interest rates will fall, they should borrow floating. However, they may subsequently decide that they have made the wrong decision. A swap allows borrowers to manage their existing debt. They can choose to swap not only from fixed to floating or vice versa but also from one currency to another.

Now that there is a secondary market in swaps, borrowers can reverse their swap decisions if they wish. Say a borrower had swapped from borrowing fixed to borrowing floating when interest rates were 12 per cent and that rates subsequently dropped to 8 per cent. That swap would now have a value because the borrower is receiving 12 per cent from its counterparty but paying only 8 per cent. The first borrower could sell the swap or arrange another swap by which it would agree to pay a fixed rate of 8 per cent and receive a floating rate. Its floating-rate payment under the first swap would be cancelled out by the second swap. However, it would have cut its fixed-rate payments from 12 to 8 per cent.

How are banks involved in swap deals? Some act as swap principals, agreeing to switch into fixed or floating debt or into another currency as the borrower requires. Normally, such banks have a 'book' of swaps, and they may find that their positions over a number of different swap deals balance each other out. Other banks act purely as swap arrangers, bringing together two different companies with corresponding needs: they earn fees in the process. A third set of banks follows a compromise strategy, acting as principals in a deal until they can find a matching borrower.

Swaps are off-balance-sheet transactions – they are not regarded as assets, and banks are currently not obliged to take precautions against the possibility of default. However, regulatory authorities have shown their concern about the growth of the market. Many poor credits are involved, since swaps give them the opportunity to reduce the cost of borrowing. If swap parties do default, banks may be faced with the payment of above-market interest rates.

What swaps have done is to open up the world's capital markets to a wide range of borrowers. It is now possible for a UK borrower, say, to pick a particular world market where borrowing seems cheap, borrow there and still, through a swap, end up with the sterling debt it really wants.

SPECIAL BOND ISSUES

In addition to the above instruments, borrowers have issued bonds which are designed to be more attractive to investors because they offer protection against adverse interest-rate movements. Many of these bonds are described in Chapter 10.

One type of bond issue deserves treatment here because it closely resembles a swap. The *capped floater* offers investors a floating rate set at a margin above LIBOR. However, if LIBOR rates go above a certain level, the bond rates do not follow. A 'cap' is set, which is the maximum rate the issuer will pay. The investor is compensated for the cap because the bond pays a higher than usual margin over LIBOR.

The issuer sells the cap to another borrower which wishes to lock in a maximum cost for its borrowings. The bond issuer can invest the money received from the sale of the cap, so that it receives a stream of payments which it can offset against the higher than usual margin over LIBOR that it is paying on the bond issue. This effectively can bring the cost of the issue to below LIBOR. So the issuer ends up paying less than LIBOR; the investor receives a higher than usual margin *above* LIBOR; and the cap buyer receives protection against a rise in interest rates.

After an initial surge the number of capped floaters declined. Instead banks now sell a product known as a 'cap' separately from specific bond issues. Such caps are effectively long-term interest-rate options and give the buyer the right to borrow at a specific rate. The bond market is for ever ingenious, however, and it is safe to predict that issues will be designed with a similar clever mix of fixed and floating payments in the future.

All the above instruments deal with interest-rate risk. However, the risk that currencies will move is important to both borrowers and investors and also to businesses which export and import. It is that risk we shall examine in the next chapter.

Foreign Exchange

Look into a foreign-exchange dealing room and you will often see pandemonium. Dealers hang on two or three telephone calls at a time and bellow instructions across the room. Thirty years ago dealing rooms were much more sedate. Why? The growth in the foreign-exchange markets is due not just to the increased speed of movement of international capital or even to the growth of international trade. It is due to the decline of the old system of fixed exchange rates and its replacement by floating currencies. Exchange rates now move by amounts which can wipe out profit margins and render investments virtually worthless, and the foreign-exchange markets in London can conduct many hundreds of billions worth of trades each day as investors and traders try to keep up with market moves. With so much money flowing through the system, exchange rates have become even more volatile. Since 1979 sterling, for example, has risen from $1.80 to $2.40, dropped to $1.03 and risen again to nearly $2 and fallen back to $1.45.

Currency volatility affects everyone, from the biggest multinational to the humblest tourist. Every overseas trade deal involves foreign-exchange decisions. First the people involved must agree which currency should be used to settle the deal. If one party is from Japan and the other from Switzerland, should the transaction take place in yen, Swiss francs or some other currency such as the US dollar? Equally important, when should the currency be delivered? Just as the price of the goods being sold is central to the transaction, so the exchange rate (which is the price of one currency in terms of another) can determine whether the parties make a profit or a loss.

BRETTON WOODS AND AFTER: THE ROLE OF FORECASTING TODAY

The post-war system of fixed exchange rates was set up in 1944 at an international conference held in Bretton Woods, New Hampshire. Although not fully operational until 1958, the Bretton Woods system pegged the world's major currencies at fixed rates to the dollar. In turn the dollar was given the strength to act as the linchpin of the world's financial system because of its 'convertibility', at a set rate, into gold.

Gradually the system broke down as the American economy ran into trouble because of President Johnson's attempts to finance the Vietnam war and his 'Great Society' reforms at the same time. By 1971 the dollar lacked the strength to support the system, and President Nixon announced the suspension of the dollar's convertibility into gold. A series of attempts to shore up the system failed; eventually it proved impossible to fix the value of the major currencies against the dollar.

The assumption that lay behind the fixed-rate system was that if one country had an excessive current-account deficit, it would alter its domestic economic policies until balance was restored. The system was capable of surviving the occasional hiccup, such as the sterling devaluation in 1967. However, since the system hinged on the dollar, a US balance-of-payments crisis was a more mortal wound.

Thanks to President Johnson's attempt to pay for both guns and butter, the USA developed enormous current-account deficits which it proved unable to rectify. As a result, the foreign-exchange markets were overloaded with dollars ($1 billion a day flowed into the Bundesbank in May 1971). Speculators had a one-way bet. If they sold dollars and bought a strong currency such as the Deutschmark, they were highly unlikely to lose money, but if the dollar devalued, they would make substantial gains.

The enormous scale of international capital flows today means that no central bank has the reserves to defend its currency against market speculation indefinitely. As a consequence, a Bretton Woods-type system is unlikely ever to return.

Why have exchange rates been so unstable since the collapse of the Bretton Woods system? Many theories have been developed to explain why exchange rates change, but none has so far explained their movements in such a way that future exchange-rate moves can then be predicted with any degree of accuracy.

Economic theories attempt to explain exchange-rate moves in the long run. Foreign-exchange dealers have to predict exchange rates in the very short run indeed – a day or two at the most. Companies whose profits are hurt or boosted by currency movements often need to know about the medium term – between two months and a year or so. When they turn to currency forecasters they are often disappointed. Surveys of foreign-exchange analysts regularly come to the conclusion that the forecasters are right in less than half of their predictions – a record worse than might be expected from tossing a coin.

There are two schools of currency forecasters – the economists and the technical analysts – and their methods are radically different. The economists have academic respectability and intellectual recognition. Sometimes, however, the technical analysts have the greater influence in the market.

THE ECONOMISTS

Because the system of fixed exchange rates survived for so long, economic theories about exchange rates have been developed from earlier studies about the way in which the balance of payments changes.

The most important initial distinction to make is that between the current and capital accounts of the balance of payments. The *current account* broadly covers trade payments, although it also includes tourist expenditure and, most important, interest payments and dividends. The *capital account* is concerned largely with purchases of assets – foreign securities such as German bonds, Japanese shares or physical assets like a factory in the Philippines. Note that purchase of a foreign bond counts as a debit on the capital account, but interest on the bond will be shown as a credit on the current account. The notion of a balance of payments is that a surplus or deficit of a current account will be balanced by a deficit or surplus on the capital account.

If, under the fixed-rate exchange system, a country was in current-account deficit, then to pay for the excess goods and services that it received from abroad it would have to act to correct the deficit. Trade barriers were ruled out under the General Agreement on Tariffs and

Trade (GATT), so the country would be obliged to run down its foreign physical and financial assets or to borrow abroad in order to pay for its imports. In either case the inflow would be recorded as a capital-account surplus that matched the current-account deficit.

In the long term a deficit government was expected to curb demand in the economy, so that domestic consumers cut back their expenditure on both domestic and foreign goods. The price of domestic goods would fall in response to this drop in demand, making them more attractive to foreign consumers and pushing up the country's exports. Since imports would fall (because domestic consumers could not afford to buy them), the net effect would be to restore the balance-of-payments equilibrium. According to this model, devaluation would occur only when a country had run down its reserves so far that it was unable to restore current-account balance at the prevailing exchange rate.

The above example assumes that the capital account is not an independent variable but responds only to changes in the current account. In fact, the international flows of capital mean that the capital account is very much at the mercy of investor demand for foreign and domestic securities. As we saw, this was one of the reasons why the fixed exchange-rate system did not survive.

In the era of floating rates, economists have attempted to study how the exchange rate affects, and is affected by, both the current and the capital account. Their study has centred on two factors, the level of prices and the level of interest rates.

The study of the effect of prices on exchange rates has focused on the purchasing power parity (PPP) theory. At its simplest the theory argues that exchange rates will tend towards the point at which international purchasing power is equal. In other words, a hamburger would cost the same in any country. In turn that means that differential inflation rates are the most important driving factor behind exchange-rate movements.

Inflation matters because high prices make a country's goods uncompetitive. If the UK's inflation is 10 per cent per annum while the USA's is zero, British goods will be 10 per cent more expensive than American goods after a year has elapsed. Unless British productivity outpaces that of the USA by 10 per cent, UK sales abroad will fall as customers find it cheaper to buy American or other alternatives, and UK imports will increase as domestic consumers prefer US goods to their own. Hence the current account will deteriorate.

This sorry picture, PPP theorists claim, is redeemed by the exchange rate. If the pound falls by 10 per cent against the dollar in the above example, the cost to the US customer of UK goods (in dollars) stays the same. Similarly, the dollar has risen by 10 per cent, and therefore the cost to the US customer of American goods (in pounds) is the same. So the exchange rate has acted to restore the balance.

Monetarists have adopted and modified this theory. They believe that price increases are caused by an excess money supply. Thus, since the markets know that nations with slack monetary regimes will suffer inflation, they will sell the currency of that country and buy the currency of countries with stricter monetary control. The resulting exchange-rate depreciation will in the long run match the differential in money-supply growth between the two countries. Unless money-supply growth is checked, the process of inflation-provoked devaluation will continue.

The concept of an equilibrium level for exchange rates has given PPP theorists a lot of trouble. There is no point of zero inflation and equilibrium currency rates from which subsequent exchange-rate movements can be measured. A base year must therefore be chosen, and the choice of base year often determines whether an exchange rate appears under- or overvalued. The years of rampant Western inflation, 1974–8, are a particular source of problems.

Another major difficulty with the PPP theory is deciding what is defined by inflation. If the price of hairdressing is included in the consumer price index (CPI), will that make the index a reasonable measure of UK competitiveness? How many Americans will cross the Atlantic to get a cheaper perm? More seriously, an important component of any CPI is housing costs, which are irrelevant to consideration of export competitiveness. Even wholesale prices cover items that are not internationally traded. The most popular measure of competitiveness has therefore been unit wage costs – that is, the amount paid to workers per unit of output.

The PPP theory holds out very well for many Third World countries, in particular Latin American where exchange-rate depreciation against the dollar tends to follow the inflation rate quite closely. When it comes to predicting and explaining the exchange-rate movements of the currencies of the major industrialized countries, however, it has been less successful.

If PPP theory is correct, real exchange rates (nominal exchange rates adjusted for inflation) should stay fairly stable. In fact, research has demonstrated that real rates show considerable volatility and exhibit little sign of returning to any equilibrium level. Some explain this by the concept of 'overshooting', in which because of market inefficiencies, exchange rates over-adjust in response to inflationary differentials. If they do, that makes it all the more difficult to use PPP theory as an exchange-rate predictor.

The level of interest rates is clearly a major factor in the strength or weakness of a currency. This is even more the case after the recent wave of financial deregulation which we noted in Chapter 1. The world is now virtually a single capital market, in which vast quantities of money shift from one country to another in search of short-term gains.

The influence of interest rates is not as easy to assess as might first be thought. To begin with, are investors attracted by the nominal rate or the real rate (the nominal rate adjusted for inflation)? Second, are high interest rates a sign of a healthy or of an ailing economy?

For a long time foreign-exchange speculators perceived currencies in high-interest economies as weak and currencies in low-interest economies as strong. If a currency were weak, the argument went, few people would want to hold it or lend it, since currency depreciation would soon reduce its value. Debtors would want their borrowings denominated in a weak currency, however, since currency depreciation would reduce their debt burden. As a result there would be few lenders and many borrowers in that currency. In other words, demand for borrowings would exceed the supply and thus force the interest rate up.

The converse would apply to strong currencies. Many people would want to hold or lend them, since, added to the interest received would be the extra value gained from the currency's appreciation. On the other hand, few would want their debts denominated in a strong currency, since currency appreciation would keep increasing the effective total of their debt. In a strong currency, therefore, there would be many lenders and few borrowers. The supply of borrowings would exceed demand, forcing the interest rate down. That analysis has been overtaken by the influence of monetarism.

Monetarist economists have argued that high interest rates are often a good sign in an economy, since they restrict demand for credit and therefore reduce the chances of inflation. Low interest rates imply slack control of credit and therefore the possibility of inflationary pressures.

The position has been complicated further by the willingness of governments to push their interest rates up in order to defend their currencies. Take the desperate attempts of the UK to prop up the pound in September 1992. The then Chancellor Norman Lamont was forced to increase interest rates twice in one day from 10 to 12 per cent, and then to 15 per cent, in an attempt to keep sterling within its Exchange Rate Mechanism band. But high interest rates impose a heavy burden on the economy, in terms of lost jobs and output, and few traders believed the UK government would sustain rates at that level. The pound fell anyway, and the UK was forced out of the ERM.

What most economists now think is that the key factor in determining capital inflow is the expected real interest rate – in other words, the return that the investor expects to receive after inflation and exchange rates have been taken into account. Even if nominal interest rates are high, investors will not buy investments in a country if they think that currency depreciation or inflation will wipe out their return. What determines those expectations is hard to define. But the dollar's overwhelming strength in 1983 and 1984 seemed to depend on investors' expectations that the Reagan administration and the Federal Reserve would keep US interest rates high and inflation low.

The latest and most cogent economic theory of exchange-rate movements is the portfolio balance model.* Proponents of this theory argue that exchange rates are effectively the relative prices of international financial assets (e.g. bonds and shares). It is expectations of the likely risk and return of financial assets that determine exchange-rate movements as investors shift their portfolios from one country to another.

The portfolio balance theory is persuasive partly because capital flows are far larger than trade flows. Another reason is that major economic or political events have an effect on the financial markets much more quickly than they do on the prices of goods. Bond prices move almost constantly, thanks to the electronic communications systems: the prices of goods change more slowly and depend on many factors. The combination of trade and capital flows results in the erratic paths of exchange rates as the two factors act sometimes in the same direction and sometimes in opposite directions.

Currency movements thus seem to depend to a large extent on the

* I am very grateful to David Morrison for his explanation of this theory.

subjective views of those involved in the international capital markets. This concentration on expectation has given a great boost to the other strand of currency forecasters – the technical analysts.

TECHNICAL ANALYSIS

Technical analysts, or 'chartists' as they are often known, believe that all the factors which the economist studies – inflation, the balance of payments, interest rates, etc. – are already known by the market and are thus reflected in the prices of goods and commodities. This is as true of pork bellies and oil as it is of currencies. The chartists, as their name suggests, study charts which represent the price movements of a particular commodity. Over long periods certain price patterns emerge, which cause the analysts to claim that further developments in the price pattern can be predicted.

Economists have a tendency to reject the chartist theories out of hand. However, many traders in the foreign-exchange markets follow the chartists' predictions. To some extent such predictions can become self-fulfilling if enough people believe them. The markets react when a certain point of the chart is reached.

The underlying rationale behind chart analysis is that the key to price movements is human reaction, and that human nature does not change markedly in response to similar events. Among the main patterns that chartists see are the following.

Head and shoulders. This pattern is made up of a major rise in price (the head) separating two smaller rises (the shoulders). If this pattern is established, the price should fall by the same amount as the distance between the head and a line connecting the bottom of the two shoulders.

Broadening top. This pattern has three price peaks at successively higher levels and, between them, two bottoms with the second one lower than the first. If, after the third peak, the price falls below the level of the second bottom, this indicates a major reversal in the price trend.

Double bottoms/tops. A double bottom or top indicates a major reversal in the price trend. Both consist of two troughs (or peaks) separated by a price movement in the opposite direction.

Apart from pattern recognition, technical analysts also study *momentum* and *moving average* models. *Momentum* analysis studies the rate of change of prices rather than merely price levels. If the rate of change is increasing, that indicates that a trend will continue; if the rate of change is decreasing, that indicates that the trend is likely to be reversed. The concept behind the study of *moving averages* is that trends in price movements last long enough to allow shrewd investors to profit and that rules can be discovered which identify the most important of these trends. One of the most significant rules for technical analysts is that a major shift has occurred when a long-term moving average crosses a short-term moving average.

Although technical analysis has very little intellectual respectability in economists' circles, it has had a great impact on the foreign-exchange markets. Many believe it to be a useful forecasting tool in the short term. In the long term, despite some setbacks, economic analysis may yet prove a more successful forecasting technique.

THE EUROPEAN SINGLE CURRENCY

The foreign-exchange markets are currently witnessing one of the great economic experiments of all time – the creation of the European single currency, or euro.

European governments struggled for a long time with the break-up of the Bretton Woods system. By nature, they were less inclined to embrace floating exchange rates than the more laissez-faire economies of the UK and the US and the subsequent 25 years saw a series of attempts to restrict currency movements.

The first attempt in the mid 1970s – the 'snake' – collapsed fairly quickly and the second attempt – the Exchange Rate Mechanism – was plagued by repeated crises between 1979 and 1983.

Change started to occur when the French government decided to aim for a strong currency, or *franc fort*. This made it easier for the franc to stabilize against the established currency of Europe, the Deutschmark, and removed some of the tensions within the system.

But in the early 1990s, the ERM broke down. The catalyst was the reunification of Germany which created inflationary pressures that the German central bank, the Bundesbank, decided to tackle by increasing interest rates. To maintain their parity against the Deutschmark, other currencies within the system had to increase their interest rates, driving some economies into recession.

Some countries, including Britain but also Italy, could not stand the strain. They eventually opted in 1992 for the less painful option of devaluation and interest rate cuts. One year later, speculative attacks looked like forcing the French franc to devalue; in the event the ERM was changed to allow much wider trading bands, which were close enough to floating rates as to make no difference.

The break-up of the ERM created the impetus for the drive towards a single currency. The Maastricht Treaty (from which Britain had an opt-out) established the criteria which companies needed to meet; including annual budget deficits less than 3 per cent of gross domestic product and inflation rates close to the European average.

The process for preparation went rather more smoothly than sceptics might have expected. There were no speculative attacks in the last days of the old system; interest rates and bond yields in the higher-risk countries, such as Italy and Spain, smoothly came down to German levels.

At the start of 1999, European exchange rates were 'locked in' at set levels against the euro and it became possible to use the currency for commercial transactions. Notes and coins duly arrived at the start of 2002, at which point the old currencies of the 12 member countries – Germany, France, Belgium, Luxembourg, Netherlands, Ireland, Spain, Austria, Portugal, Finland, Italy and Greece – ceased to exist.

A single currency will bring a number of advantages. First it will remove a level of uncertainty when European companies do business with each other; they will no longer have to worry that exchange-rate movements will eat into their profits.

Second, it should reduce the costs of doing business within the continent. Every time money is converted from one currency into another, there are commission and dealing costs to be paid.

Third, it should make markets more efficient. It will make it easier for Europeans to compare prices in different countries and to buy from the cheapest supplier.

Against all this is the lack of flexibility which will result. One currency means one interest rate for the whole continent, no matter what the economic conditions in each country. So Ireland, growing at 7 to 8 per cent a year, was cutting interest rates in late 1998, instead of raising them as economic theory would suggest.

Should a European country face recession in future years, when the rest of the continent is buoyant, it will not have the option of devaluation or cutting rates. Nor will it be able to revive its economy through a wave of public spending; a so-called stability pact puts limits on budget deficits.

Of course, the US is a big country, with one currency and interest rate. But it has a fairly mobile population; if one region is depressed, workers can quickly move to another. Language makes that option a lot harder for Europeans.

Britain has yet to join the euro at the time of writing. Government policy is to call a referendum if five (rather vague) economic tests are met. Britons will have to weigh the economic pros and cons of such a move, but many seem to be opposed on principle, arguing against the loss of sovereignty involved. If Britain were to join the single currency, interest rates would be set at the European Central Bank's headquarters in Frankfurt.

The first three years of the euro's life did not do much to advance the case of sterling entry. The euro was weak against the US dollar and the European Central Bank was perceived as being clumsy in its handling of the market. The Bank of England, in contrast, earned praise for its ability to combat inflation without jeopardizing economic growth.

EMERGING MARKET CURRENCIES

The problems of dealing with floating exchange rates have not been confined to the countries of Europe. The so-called emerging markets, the developing nations of Asia, Latin America and eastern Europe, have also grappled with the issue.

Economic problems have a habit of showing up in exchange rate movements. In Latin America, historically high inflation rates caused massive depreciations of currencies against the dollar, particularly in the 1980s. Then in 1994, the Mexican government was prompted into devaluing the peso in the face of a massive trade deficit.

Asian countries had traditionally produced much better economic performances than Latin America and their consequences had tradition- ally been stronger. But then in 1997, Thailand suddenly devalued its currency, the baht, triggering a wave of devaluations round the region.

Asia's apparent strength had hidden some underlying weaknesses. Many countries had linked their currencies, formally and informally, to the dollar, encouraging many companies to take out US dollar loans because of the lower interest rates in America. Furthermore, their reputations as fast-growing economies had resulted in a massive influx of capital, much of which had been invested at economically unfeasible rates. In short, a speculative bubble had been created.

When sentiment turned, the bubble burst very quickly. The hot money that had flowed into the Asian countries flowed out again; as the currencies depreciated, the burden of meeting the corporate system's dollar debts became oppressive. Asian banks, which had lent heavily to the corporate sector, saw their finances deteriorate in the face of bad debts.

Many south-east Asian economies plunged into recession; the IMF was called in to provide rescue financing packages. The whole issue cast doubt on the 'Asian economic miracle' and prompted a lot of debate about free market regimes.

Some countries and commentators argued that the system showed the instability of global capitalism, and the need for controls; Malaysia duly imposed capital controls in 1998. Free market enthusiasts argued that it was the attempts of governments to track the dollar and their interference in the free running of their economies which caused the problem.

THE FOREIGN-EXCHANGE MARKET

Participants in the foreign-exchange market include everyone from the Governor of the Bank of England to tourists when they buy foreign currency for a holiday. Tourist purchases are, in fact, among the few foreign-exchange transactions in which notes and coins actually change hands. The vast majority of deals take place over the telephone in bank dealing rooms, and funds are transferred electronically from one account to another.

At the core of the market are the banks. Most commercial banks have their own foreign-exchange room. Although banks could not deal if they were not providing a service for their corporate clients who need foreign exchange as part of their everyday business, the majority of any bank's deals are done with other banks. One bank has estimated that 95 per cent of its foreign-exchange business is done with other banks and only 5 per cent with outside customers.

There are three major dealing time zones, all of which have more than one centre. London was considered the most important centre, although New York has now probably taken over that role. The market begins each day at 1 a.m. Greenwich Mean Time (GMT), when Tokyo opens. The Far Eastern time zone holds sway until 9 a.m. GMT, by which time London, Frankfurt, Paris and Zurich have begun the European time-zone trading. By 2 p.m. GMT, New York has opened trading in the American time zone. The market does not close in New York until 10 p.m. GMT. Those dealers who are still awake can trade in San Francisco and Los Angeles until Tokyo opens the next day.

With so many markets to keep track of, the pace of a dealer's life is often frenetic. Most are young, and some are burnt out by their middle thirties. How do they operate?

Suppose a dealer gets a commercial request to buy or sell a large volume of currency. He has several choices. He can satisfy the request himself or ask one of his colleagues to do so. If his colleague cannot, he can ring up a dealer in another bank and hope that he will be able to sell on the currency to his counterpart. But this can be time-consuming. His alternative is to contact a foreign-exchange broker, whose job is to find a willing counterparty to the deal. In return for this service, the broker charges a commission, which can be as small as one-hundredth of 1 per cent. However, one-hundredth of 1 per cent of deals worth £1 million a time can quickly add up to a lot of money.

The broker will always attempt to cover his position; in other words, he will ensure that he is selling and buying the same amount of currency, so that he is safeguarded against fluctuation. Dealers will usually do the same, although they are allowed, within limits, to leave surplus funds in currencies which they believe will appreciate.

An exchange of currencies for immediate delivery is conducted at the *spot* rate. Dealers will quote two exchange rates for each currency, one at which they will buy the currency and one at which they will sell. The difference between the two is one way in which a bank makes money and is called the *spread*. So if you wanted to buy dollars in exchange for sterling, the bank might offer $1.4850/£1. If you had wanted to buy sterling in exchange for dollars, the rate would have been $1.4870/£1. (For brevity the sterling/dollar rate would be given by a dealer as 50/70.) The 0.2 cent difference between the two rates is the spread. These rates are displayed and continually updated throughout the day in foreign-exchange dealing rooms and on Reuters screens, and they appear every day in the *Financial Times*. The faster an exchange rate is moving, the wider the spread, since the dealer will not want to be committed to dealing at an unfavourable rate.

Tourists buying foreign currencies will find that the spread is very wide, often several percentage points. Banks can afford to charge each other a narrow spread because the deals are large and frequent and because the competition is intense. The tourist, by comparison, has little bargaining power, and the bank's costs in supplying the small amounts of currencies involved are proportionately higher.

THE FORWARD RATE

Banks will quote a price for a currency which is not wanted for immediate delivery. If a UK company knows that it is going to receive goods from Switzerland in three months' time, for which it will have to pay Swiss francs, it can fix its exchange rate in advance by locking in a forward rate with a bank. If the spot rate is Sfr 2.2568/72 per £1, the bank might offer a three-month forward rate of Sfr 2.2291/97 per £1. Once again the bank is taking a spread – notice that the spread for the three-month forward rate is larger than for the spot rate. On screen the bank will in fact show only the differential between the spot and forward rates. So in this case the screen would show:

Rates against the £

	Spot	Forward
Swiss franc	2.2568/72	277/275

Currencies that are more expensive to obtain at the forward rate than at the spot rate are described as being at a *premium*, and those that are cheaper on the forward than on the spot market are at a *discount*. In this case, the Swiss franc is at a premium to the pound and the pound is at a discount to the franc. On a dealer's screen the distinction is shown by the ordering of the forward's spread. As the Swiss franc is at a premium to the pound, the largest figure appears first in the forward column. If the Swiss franc were at a discount, the forward column would read 275/277.

Forward rates are determined largely by interest differentials. Imagine that Swiss interest rates were 10 per cent and UK rates were 5 per cent and that the spot and the twelve-month forward rates for Swiss francs against sterling were the same. A UK investor would then be able to buy Swiss francs at the spot rate and invest the money in Switzerland to earn the higher interest rate. At the same time the investor could take out a forward contract with a bank to buy back sterling in exchange for Swiss francs in a year's time. No money would be lost as a result of currency movements, since the investor has guaranteed the same Swiss franc/ sterling rate as when the investment was made. So the investor could benefit from higher Swiss interest rates without risk. This method of profiting from inconsistencies between markets is known as *arbitrage*.

Attractive though it may seem, the above example could not happen in the real world. Every investor would be anxious to profit from the trade. The result would be: (a) increased demand from UK investors for Swiss francs at the spot rate, driving the Swiss franc up against sterling; (b) increased demand for Swiss and reduced demand for UK assets, driving Swiss interest rates down and UK rates up; (c) increased demand for twelve-month sterling, driving the twelve-month Swiss franc rate down and thus opening up a differential with the spot rate, which would be pushed in the opposite direction. All these factors combined would quickly eliminate the investment opportunity described.

Although arbitrage possibilities do sometimes exist and some speculators make a living out of exploiting them, the speed of the markets means that inconsistencies do not last very long. A country which has higher interest rates than those in the UK will have a currency at a discount to the pound on the forward market, so that investors would lose on the currency what they would gain on the interest-rate differential. By contrast, countries with lower interest rates than the UK's will have currencies at a premium to sterling.

THE COMPANY'S DILEMMA

Any company involved in overseas trade has to face the problems described in the introductory paragraphs of this chapter. Which currency should it choose to pay or be paid in, and when should it arrange for that currency to be delivered?

The volatility of the foreign-exchange market is such that currency moves can wipe out profit margins and render companies bankrupt. Suppose a US company had made a five-year investment denominated in sterling in 1981, when the dollar sterling rate was $2.40/£1. By early 1985 the rate had fallen to $1.10/£1. The investment would have had to double in value to eliminate the currency-depreciation effect.

To counter these problems many companies have a set policy for choosing the denominating currency for their transactions. Often this policy will be to trade always in the currency of the country in which the firm is based, in an attempt to eliminate currency risk altogether. This policy works very well until the company attempts to deal with another firm with the same policy but in a different country. It is also very unlikely that a UK company would accept payment in, say, Venezuelan bolivars because of the difficulty of converting the currency when delivered.

For these reasons the majority of international trade is denominated in dollars. Not only is the US unit freely convertible but it is also used by many governments as a reserve currency. Since such a large proportion of their business is done in dollars, companies can match up their payments and receipts to reduce their foreign-exchange risk, using the dollars received from sales to pay for supplies.

If a company cannot arrange to pay or be paid either in dollars or in its native currency, its best option is to ask to be paid in some other strong currency. The euro may yet develop to challenge the dollar as the currency of choice. Multinational companies, which usually have to cope with a wide variety of currencies, will attempt to match their payments and receipts in all of the units in which they have transactions in order to keep their total exchange risk to a minimum.

Once a transaction in a particular currency has been arranged, how does a company cope with the foreign-exchange risk involved? Most companies think that their business is trading and not currency speculation, so they will try to avoid risk as much as possible. Suppose a UK company is due to receive dollars three months ahead. It has a number of choices.

First, it could wait for three months, receive the dollars and exchange them for sterling on the spot market. If, in the meantime, the dollar has appreciated against the pound, the company has made money; if the dollar has fallen, the company has lost money.

Second, it could arrange a forward transaction with a bank to sell dollars three months ahead or to buy a dollar-denominated deposit which matures in three months' time. The company's treasurer can sleep at night; the firm is protected against a dollar collapse. But if the dollar rises, the firm will find itself getting a great deal less for its dollars than it might have done.

Third, a middle position: the company could assess which way it thinks the dollar will move. Say it feels there is a 50 per cent chance that it will get a better dollar rate three months ahead than by using the forward market. It therefore sells enough dollars forward to cover 50 per cent of its total position and waits to buy the rest on the spot market. Total disaster has been avoided, and there is the chance of profiting if the dollar rises.

In recent years more and more companies have shown a preference for taking a fourth possible course of action – buying a currency option.

CURRENCY OPTIONS

Currency options are similar to the interest-rate options described in Chapter 12. They give the buyer the right, but not the obligation, to buy foreign currency at a specified rate. Thus the buyer is protected against an adverse exchange-rate movement but retains the potential to take advantage of any favourable movement.

Suppose that a UK company is committed to paying US dollars for oil in three months' time. It is worried that sterling will fall during that period, thus forcing up the cost of the oil. Sterling is at that moment $1.20 on the spot market. So the company buys a three-month sterling put option (the right to sell sterling in exchange for dollars) at a strike price of $1.20. If, during the life of the option, sterling falls to $1.10, the company exercises its option and sells sterling at the more favourable rate of $1.20. However, if sterling rises to $1.30, then the company allows the option to lapse and sells sterling (and buys dollars) on the spot market.

The catch is the cost. The option buyer must pay the seller a premium when the option is purchased. That premium is non-returnable and is considerably larger than the cost of using the forward market. The option seller charges more than for forward cover because of the higher risk involved. An option can be exercised at any time before its expiry date, and that means that the seller must be constantly prepared to exchange currency at an unfavourable rate. In the forward market, however, the day and the rate at which currencies will be exchanged are known in advance.

Although the option buyer pays more, it is for a better product than forward cover. If the UK company in the example above had covered its risk by buying a three-month forward contract at $1.21, it would have been unable to benefit from a move in the spot rate to $1.30 and might well have ended up paying more for its oil than its competitors. It is also important to remember that the premium represents the maximum possible cost to the option buyer.

Let us take another example. An American company wishes to buy Swiss goods. The company negotiates a price of Sfr 1,250,000, which it must pay in three months' time. The spot rate is $0.73 per Sfr. The forward rate is 0.74 per Sfr. The premium of a $0.73 option is $0.015 per Sfr.

SCENARIO A

The spot rate moves to Sfr 0.76.
If the company does nothing, the cost of goods is:
Sfr 1,250,000 × 0.7600 = $950,000.
If the company buys forward, the cost of goods is:
Sfr 1,250,000 × 0.74 = $925,000.
If the company buys an option and exercises it, the cost of goods is:
Sfr 1,250,000 × 0.73 = $912,500,
plus cost of premium
Sfr 1,250,000 × 0.015 = $18,750.
Total = $931,250.

SCENARIO B

The spot price moves to Sfr 0.70.
If the company does nothing, the cost of goods is:
Sfr 1,250,000 × 0.70 = $875,000.
If the company buys forward, the cost of goods is:
Sfr 1,250,000 × 0.74 = $925,000.
If the company buys an option and does not exercise it, the cost of goods is:
Sfr 1,250,000 × 0.70 = $875,000,
plus cost of premium
Sfr 1,250,000 × 0.015 = $18,750.
Total = $893,750.

In both scenarios the option outperforms the worst strategy but does not perform as well as the best strategy. This makes options very attractive to many companies, which see them as a form of insurance covering foreign risk rather than fire or theft.

Most companies buy options direct from banks (over-the-counter options – OTCs). However, it is also possible to buy and sell options on futures exchanges such as the LIFFE (the London International Financial Futures Exchange). Traded options are for standardized amounts and time periods and are available only in a limited number of currencies. However, the premiums are generally cheaper than those of OTC options.

CURRENCY FUTURES

Currency futures are priced in dollars per foreign currency unit. (For example, a sterling contract on a Chicago futures exchange might be priced at $1.10 per £1.) Contract sizes are quite small to accommodate the small speculators who give futures exchanges their liquidity.

Those who use currency futures can be divided into two groups: *speculators* and *hedgers*. *Speculators* act on a hunch that currencies are moving in a particular direction. If they believe that the dollar is going to fall against sterling, then they buy sterling futures in the hope that the value of these will appreciate. *Hedgers* will already be committed to a foreign-exchange position and will buy or sell enough futures contracts to ensure that their initial position is cancelled out.

Suppose a US company is due to pay out £100,000 in three months' time. Its worry is that sterling may rise against the dollar over that period. So it buys four sterling futures contracts, each worth £25,000. The prevailing sterling exchange rate is $1.10. If sterling rises to $1.25, the company will find itself paying out $115,000, $5,000 more than it would have paid if the exchange rate had stayed the same. But the futures contracts will have increased in value by the same amount. The company will have covered its losses.

As explained in Chapter 12, the system of margin payments allows users of futures contracts to insure against the risks of currency movements without actually exchanging the nominal amount of the contract.

14 Personal Finance

Individuals have a wide range of options when considering savings and investments and the thorough reader should seek professional advice before investing a large sum. There is rarely a perfect answer to an individual's investment requirements. It is wise to remember that even professional advisers make investment mistakes and they have a lot of time and resources with which to investigate and analyse the market. All this chapter can do is indicate the range of investments on offer to the individual and their advantages and disadvantages.

The rules which govern the finances of individuals are not much different from the ones that govern the finance of institutions. There is still a trade-off between liquidity and reward. The deposit account which gives the customer the best interest rate may impose penalties for early withdrawals of money. There is also the same trade-off between risk and reward. Those investments which offer the best return – shares, options, etc. – also involve the possibility of loss. The safest investments offer a steady but unspectacular return.

Investments can also appear safe when they are not. In the 1980s, those who invested money with a firm called Barlow Clowes thought, erroneously, that they were opting for the safe haven of gilts. They learnt that the choice of investment manager can be just as important as the choice of investment.

So before investors sign away their hard-earned savings, they should consider carefully what they expect from their investments. Might they want to withdraw their money early to pay for a car or a holiday? What value do they place on safety? Would they rather forgo the chance of capital gain in order to avoid the possibility of capital loss? Have they a lump sum to invest or a small amount each month? Do they pay income tax and, if so, at what rate? When they have the answer to those questions, investors can examine the merits of the various investments on offer more efficiently.

At the risk of sounding very banal, there are also some very simple steps which can be as effective as months of analysis of new forms of savings accounts. A wise rule, for example, for a credit card holder is to pay off the balance at the end of every month. It is very rare for an individual to be able to earn more from his investments than he pays on his borrowings. So it is better to take money out of the building society to pay off debt.

PROPERTY

Most people make their life's main investment in property. Taking out a mortgage is a different form of investment from the others discussed in this chapter since it is an investment financed by borrowing. The other schemes discussed involve the use of money saved from income. Historically, one great advantage of investing in a house was that the interest cost was tax deductible. But successive governments have whittled away the benefit, abolishing it entirely in the 1999 Budget. At least the profit made on the sale of a homeowner's main residence is still free of capital gains tax.

Although the attractions of home ownership seem obvious, it is well to remember that house buyers are, in fact, making a complex calculation. The alternative to house buying is, of course, renting. Depending on the size of the deposit, mortgage repayments can be considerably more expensive than rents, and other items such as buildings insurance and maintenance can add to the bill. However, mortgage payments go up and down with the rate of interest and not, like rents, with the rate of inflation. So over the long term, rental payments should grow by more than the monthly mortgage.

In the past, most people saw the benefits of property investment in terms of the increase in house prices. However, as one house's price is increasing, so are the prices of all the others. When the house is sold, the next house may be even more expensive. The costs of moving are also high. Estate agents normally take 2 per cent of the price, legal costs can easily reach 1 per cent and stamp duty up to 4 per cent more, making up to 7 per cent in all. On top of those costs are the charges of removal men and the inconvenience involved.

But these difficulties were dwarfed in the early 1990s by the problem of negative equity. Most homeowners (particularly first-time buyers) own only a small proportion of their house. The rest is covered by the mortgage. The mortgage lender does not care whether the house rises or falls in price; it wants the amount of the loan to be repaid in full.

Supposing a homeowner buys a house for £100,000 with a deposit of 5 per cent and borrowing the remaining 95 per cent from a building society. If the house falls 10 per cent in value (to £90,000), the homeowner still owes the building society £95,000. But he cannot sell the house to repay the debt since he would not raise enough money. He is trapped in 'negative equity'.

The 1980s boom in prices was exceptional; normally buying a house requires a fairly long-term approach to investment. But for most people it is an investment that pays off. A tenant will pay rent for ever, while most homeowners will have paid off their mortgages by the time they have retired and their earnings have been cut. The worst time for house buyers is soon after their purchase, but, as the salary increases, the burden of a mortgage is reduced.

The house price boom of the late 1990s proved that Britons have not lost their taste for home ownership. While those who bought in 1988 have suffered, anyone who has owned a house since the early 1970s has made fantastic profits. In some areas of London, a house bought for £10,000 in the 1970s could easily sell for £300,000 to £400,000 these days.

Traditionally, building societies were the main providers of mortgages but now they share the market with banks and other lenders. This competition has meant an end to the old days of 'mortgage famine' when borrowers were forced to go cap in hand to their building society manager. Now many institutions will lend three (and even four) times an individual's annual income. If a couple are buying a house, the lower of the two incomes will be added to three times the higher (i.e. if one person earns £20,000 and the other £16,000, the possible total will be £60,000 + £16,000 = £76,000). However, most will expect the buyer to provide a deposit of around 5 to 10 per cent of the purchase price.

For amounts over 80 per cent of the value of the house, the building society will demand that the buyer insures against default by paying a one-off premium to an insurance company. Note that the building society will offer a loan, based on their valuation of the house, or the agreed sale price, *whichever is the lower*.

If the price of the house is over £60,000, stamp duty of 1 per cent is payable, rising to 3 per cent for houses worth more than £250,000 and 4 per cent for homes above £500,000.

There are different types of mortgage agreement – the best-known being the *repayment mortgage*, under which the monthly payments are structured over the lifetime of the loan so that at the end of the period both interest and capital have been repaid. Over the first few years of the mortgage, very little of the capital is repaid. This can surprise home buyers who sell their houses after a few years.

An alternative to the repayment mortgage is the *endowment mortgage*. At the same time as the borrower takes out the mortgage, he or she takes out a life assurance policy with a monthly premium payment. At the time that the mortgage ends, the insurance policy matures and repays the full amount of the loan. In the meantime, the borrower has paid interest but not capital each month to the building society. The tax benefit is thus retained throughout the life of the loan. There are two further advantages of endowment mortgages. One is that if the borrower dies, the loan will be repaid in full. The second is that the policy can be transferred from house to house as the borrower moves.

However, endowment mortgages have many disadvantages. The main one is that they are very inflexible. It is normally 25 years before the policy will be paid out in full. If the buyer abandons the policy in the first few years, he will probably get back less than he paid in. This is because the costs involved in setting up a policy are so heavy and are reclaimed from policy holders. It may be as long as 10 years before a policyholder can get back his premiums in full.

Endowment mortgages were sold very heavily in the 1970s and 1980s, pushed by salesmen who earned substantial commissions for recommending them (they earned nothing for recommending repayment mortgages). But it has become clear in recent years that future investment returns will be poor and that some endowment policies will not grow sufficiently to repay the mortgage. This has severely dented the popularity of endowments.

There are alternative ways of paying off a mortgage. A *pension mortgage* is similar in principle to an endowment mortgage. In return for extra payments, not only is the house price repaid, but a sizeable pension is accumulated. This is a particularly useful scheme for those people who are self-employed and who do not benefit from an occupational pension scheme.

Borrowers also have a choice between borrowing at a fixed and at a variable rate. In each case, you take a risk. If you borrow at a variable rate, you risk that rates might rise; if you borrow at a fixed rate, the danger is that rates may fall and you will not see the benefit. Over the course of the 1990s, the trend in interest rates was down, meaning that those who opted for variable rates tended to get the better part of the deal. But by late 2001, both the fixed and variable rates on offer were at their lowest levels for a generation; borrowers could hardly lose.

Fixed rates offer borrowers the certainty that they know what their payments will be and can budget for them. However, many lenders insist on extras, such as insurance policies, for those who take out fixed rate deals; these can add substantially to the cost. Lenders also impose redemption penalties, equivalent to several months of mortgage payments, on fixed rate deals, so it is very expensive to switch out of them.

A relatively recent addition to the list of deals is the capped mortgage. This sets a ceiling above which the rate cannot rise but allows the borrower to benefit if rates fall below that level. This deal offers the best of both worlds, protecting borrowers against a sudden surge in interest rates without locking them into an unattractive rate.

PENSIONS

The field of pensions is one of the most complex of all to cover. Everyone knows about the basic old-age pension, funded by National Insurance contributions. Few think it is adequate as a sole source of income. In addition to the basic pension, there is the SERPS (State Earnings Related Pension Scheme), which was designed to give a higher benefit to those who wish to make extra payments in return for a higher pension at the end.

A large number of people belong to company pension schemes which 'contract out' of SERPS, offering instead a private scheme, part funded by employers, part by the employees themselves. The traditional company pension scheme is known as a defined benefit plan. Such funds must be approved by the Inland Revenue and are set up as independent trusts. They provide a very good benefit for those who retire after a long period of service for one firm. The maximum benefit available is generally retirement on two-thirds of the final salary, and there are guaranteed benefits for widows or widowers (whether the staff member dies in or out of service). The majority of schemes allow employees to take part of the pensions as a tax-free lump sum. Contributions from both employers and employees are free of tax and the fund itself can accumulate tax-free.

However, defined benefit schemes represent a risk to the companies involved. They are obliged to offer a set level of pension but they have no guarantee that the pension fund will grow by enough to meet that liability. If investment returns are poor, then the employer will have to make up the shortfall. In addition, many plans now guarantee to pay pensioners a higher benefit each year, so employers face an ever-increasing liability. (The employee also faces a risk: that the company will go bust and be unable to pay the pension in full, or at all.)

Rather than face these risks, many employers now offer what are known as defined contribution plans instead (they are also known as money purchase plans). Under these, the employer does not guarantee the final payment. The employee puts money into the fund; his or her contributions are then matched by the employer. If investment returns are good, then the final pension will be high; if they are poor, then the pension will be low. This transfers the bulk of the risk from the employer to the employee.

Traditional company schemes (particularly defined benefit plans) offer a good deal to long-term employees. But they are not so good for people who move jobs often, an increasing trend in recent years. And they are clearly not available to those who are self-employed.

In the 1980s, the government introduced personal pensions, which were designed for frequent job movers and the self-employed. Like the defined contribution (DC) plans described above, personal pensions are invested in a fund; the eventual pension is entirely dependent on the performance of that fund. But the advantage is that employees can carry on making payments into the same fund, regardless of how often he or she changes jobs.

In return for the generous tax benefits (contributions are tax-deductible and the fund rolls up tax-free), the employee cannot simply receive a lump of cash on retirement. The bulk of the fund must be used to buy an annuity, which pays out an income for the rest of the pensioner's life. Annuity rates are linked to gilt yields, which means that if an employee retires when gilt yields are low, they may get a smaller pension than expected.

People who sell personal pensions get generous commissions for doing so. That helps explain the pensions mis-selling scandal when many members of sound corporate schemes were persuaded to switch into personal pensions, which have heavy costs in their early years.

If you do take out a personal pension (or join a defined contribution scheme), remember that the level of contributions is up to you. Money cannot be created out of thin air. If you want a decent income in retirement, you will have to save a sizeable chunk of your current income. You work for forty years or so, but you may be retired for thirty.

LIFE ASSURANCE

Life assurance or insurance is also one of the biggest forms of personal savings. Until 1984, life assurance premium payments were tax-free. The combination of tax advantages and small regular payments made the schemes very popular. However, the ethics of insurance salesmen have sometimes been called into question. People approached by a salesman should establish which company he or she works for. Insurance is now sold in two ways: salesmen who are tied to a particular company; or independent financial advisers, who can recommend the products of a wide variety of companies.

The drawback of a tied agent is that he is forced to sell his company's products even though there might be better products available from other companies. But using an independent financial adviser has its dangers too. Most are paid in the form of commission from the companies whose products they sell. There are many good financial services products, such as National Savings, which pay no commission at all; others, such as unit and investment trusts, pay relatively small amounts. Life insurance companies pay relatively high rates of commission.

Accordingly, there is a natural tendency for advisers to favour life insurance products. Many honestly resist this temptation; it remains nevertheless. Some advisers are now paid solely by fees from the client; this may seem more expensive, although it will probably not be since the cost of commission is passed on to the consumer. But the main advantage of a fee system is that it ensures the adviser's interests are the same as the customer's.

There are three basic types of policies. *Term policies* provide insurance against death within a specified period of years. If the insured person lives through the period, no lump sum is paid. Premiums are consequently cheap since insurance companies can rely on the iron laws of probability to determine how likely it is that a given person of a given age will die.

Whole life policies lack a specified term of benefit. Whenever the insured person dies, the insurers must pay. However, the laws of probability still apply. The insurance company will be able to calculate when it will be required to pay.

The above two forms of policies are both *insurance* policies since they provide against the risk of death. *Assurance* policies are different because the policy holder is assured of payment. One such is an endowment policy which will be paid at the end of a fixed period – or before if the insured person dies. The premiums are the highest of the various schemes but the benefits are normally the highest.

Annuities pay an annual sum from a future date until death (it can be arranged to be paid to either husband or wife until both are deceased). The premium is normally paid in the form of a lump sum. Annuities are particularly popular with couples about to retire.

SAVINGS

Leaving aside the massive investment that many people make in property and pensions, the most common investment for the small investor is in deposit-based savings products of one kind or another. These fall into three main groups: those run by building societies, banks and the government.

BUILDING SOCIETIES

The most common building society account is the instant access. It comes in a variety of forms, some with a cash card, others with merely a passbook. Generally these accounts pay low rates of interest but are still better value than keeping large sums in a bank current account.

Those who want higher rates of interest usually need to deposit larger sums and to tie up their money for a set period. A common example is the 90-day notice account, where those who want to withdraw money must give the required notice or lose 90 days of interest. Even better rates can be obtained if you are prepared to leave your money untouched for, say, a year.

However, there are exceptions to these rules. Postal accounts can pay quite high rates with relatively quick access. This is because running building society branches is a highly expensive business. A postal account avoids those costs and the building societies can pass on those savings to depositors.

Building societies have traditionally been very safe investments, although there is always some risk, particularly with the smaller groups. A deposit protection scheme safeguards 90 per cent of the first £20,000 invested.

Building societies can now pay interest without deducting tax but depositors must first fill in a form to prove they are non-taxpayers.

NATIONAL SAVINGS

An even safer investment than either the banks or the building societies is, of course, lending to the government. The main way that the government borrows from the mass of citizens is through the various National Savings schemes, which are operated through the post offices. The government offers both taxed and untaxed schemes. The untaxed schemes are mainly in the form of certificates and bonds, which are issued in batches with each issue setting its own terms. Savings certificates offer a guaranteed (fixed) rate of interest if savers deposit money for a set term and there are penalties if money is withdrawn before the certificates expire. They are normally sold in £100 units and the maximum holding is £10,000.

To protect the saver against the effects of inflation, the government has introduced index-linked certificates, sometimes called 'granny bonds' because they were designed to appeal to old-age pensioners. The formula for calculating the yield on index-linked certificates is quite complicated but gives investors inflation protection, plus interest on top. Most issues offer not only indexation but a bonus interest rate for each successive year that the certificate is held.

National Savings products have tended to vary in their appeal in line with competition from the private sector and the government's needs for cash. Many products were attractive in the early 1990s but had ceased to be so by the latter part of the decade.

Premium bonds are another form of tax-free investment open to the individual investor but the chances of getting any return at all are fairly small. In early 1993, the government revamped the scheme increasing the top prize to £1m in an attempt to compete with the National Lottery. The yield on the fund varies with the level of interest rates.

The government, as we saw in Chapters 4 and 7, also issues long-term bonds in large denominations, known as gilts. The cheapest way of buying gilts is through the Bank of England.

The Bank now operates the service which used to be known as the National Savings Stock Register. Fortunately, investors do not have to turn up at Threadneedle Street to use the service. Forms are available at most post offices. The service is postal so while the charges will be cheaper than those imposed by a stockbroker or a bank, the process is slower and investors are exposed to sudden price movements. Income is paid gross (but is taxable).

Unlike most of the other investments we have so far described, gilts offer the chance of capital gain. As we saw in Chapter 1, the prices of bonds move up and down in inverse fashion to the level of interest rates. So, it is possible to buy a gilt at £80 one year and sell it the next at £100 and earn interest in the process. It is also well to remember that gilts can fall in price as well as rise, so there is a risk which is not involved in holding a building society deposit. The best time to buy gilts is when you expect interest rates to fall. Note the distinction between the risk that the borrower will not repay, the *credit risk*, which for gilts is virtually nil, and the risk that the investment will not be profitable, the *market risk*.

Most gilts have a fixed interest rate, which varies per issue depending on the general level of rates at the time that they were issued. However, in parallel with the issue of index-linked savings certificates, the government also issues index-linked gilts, which carry a return at a certain level above the rate of inflation. Since the first index-linked gilts were issued, inflation has fallen considerably but since little seems more certain in life than the fact that inflation will rise again, index-linked gilts and savings certificates will no doubt regain their popularity.

A new area of gilt investment has opened up with the creation of gilt strips. These, as described in Chapter 7, are essentially the component parts of a gilt issue; all the interest payments and the final repayment value. Each has a fixed value and repayment date and thus can be useful for financial planning. Each strip will trade at a discount to its repayment value; a long term strip might trade at £20 to £30 per £100. The strip should gradually rise to that level (with some sharp fluctuations on the way).

Unfortunately, the tax treatment is not favourable; the annual gain on a strip is currently subject to income tax, although the investor has not received any income.

SHARES

In the 1960s and 1970s, the riskiness of share ownership, and the distortions of the tax system, contributed to a decline in the proportion of shares held by private individuals. Instead, investment institutions dominated the equity markets. In the 1980s and 1990s, privatizations, building society flotations and the ability to trade shares through the Internet have encouraged many individuals back into the stock market, albeit in a small way.

The main problem for individuals in equity investment is the risk. As the crash of 1987 amply illustrated, share prices can fall dramatically in a single day. Even if the market as a whole does not collapse, individual shares can fall very sharply and the smallest investors are usually the last to hear the news that sparks the drop. Many technology stocks fell by 90 per cent between March 2000 and September 2001, for example. It may be bad news about an individual company that causes its share price to plunge or bad news about a sector of the economy that causes a group of share prices (e.g. computer companies) to fail.

The best way of dealing with the risk of individual price falls is to spread shareholdings over a wide range of companies. This is a matter for careful judgement; obviously, buying five separate oil stocks will not protect you against a fall in the price of oil.

The problem is that the costs of dealing – the commission paid to stockbrokers, the stamp duty, and the spread between the buy and sell prices – mean that shares have to rise by several per cent just for the investor to break even. Of course, the wider the portfolio, the greater the costs. Since one should really have a portfolio of 10 to 12 stocks, the investor ought to have at least £10,000 to £12,000 to spend. He or she should also be ready to invest long term. Also, individual sectors may be more risky than others. Investing in diamond mining may give you a chance to make your fortune but you are also far more likely to lose your stake than if you had bought shares in British Telecom.

Tips and rumours can be misleading. Many investors rashly seize on a newspaper report. A story about booming coffee prices in Brazil will have been known to others long before, and the share price of coffee producers will already reflect the news. The tips given by financial journalists are often useful but not, alas, always right. Internet bulletin boards offer a new forum for tipsters but there is no reason to assume that this information is reliable. Indeed, those who own a share have every incentive to sing its praises over the Net since an increase in the number of buyers will push up the price.

Privatizations did seem to offer easy profits for the small investor. Everyone who bought shares in British Telecom did well at first. Alas, there is little left to privatize. By no means all new issues are so successful, however; those who bought shares in the flotation of Lastminute.com were sitting on losses of 90 per cent eighteen months later. The investor should read the financial press carefully before such issues. If enough publicity is favourable, then it is likely that plenty of other investors will be willing to buy. That will mean that the issue will be oversubscribed and those investors who do not get the shares they want will try to buy the shares on the Stock Exchange, bidding up the price in the process.

Experts have a further rule of thumb – take profits and cut losses. It is luck and not judgement that allows a shareholder to sell at the highest possible price. Better to be sure of a 50 per cent gain, than lose all the gain trying to get 60 per cent. On the loss side, if a share price starts plummeting experts do not hang on in the Micawberish hope that 'something will turn up'.

Another important rule of thumb is to avoid trading too much. Investing in shares is for the long term; the most successful investor in the world, Warren Buffett, holds many shares first bought in the 1970s. Every time you trade, you incur costs and this reduces your return. This is why the idea of 'day trading', living off your profits from dealing over the computer screen, makes no sense. Studies in the US show that 70 per cent of day traders lose money.

HOW TO FOLLOW SHARE PRICES

Most serious investors should buy the *Financial Times*, which carries each day a host of information about companies and the financial markets. At the back of the paper, it prints the previous day's closing share prices. The listings of companies are separated into various groups, which can help the investor to narrow down his or her choice to a particular industry or field.

In the first column is the name of the company. Special symbols indicate factors about the company, such as the tradability of the shares. The price column shows the mid-price at the end of the previous day. This is not necessarily the price you will get if you buy or sell the shares. Traders quote different prices for buying and selling and make a profit on the spread between them.

So if a share is quoted at 100p, the price which you may have to pay to buy would be 102p, while the price you might get if you wanted to sell would be 98p.

The next column to the right shows the share price change on the day. Moving across we find the high and low for the year. Next to that is a column headed Volume '000s. This shows the level of business conducted during the previous day. It can be a useful means of checking whether a share price fall or rise is 'serious', or simply the effect of a rogue trade. Heavy volume is an indication that something may be going on at the company – whether it is a takeover approach or a forthcoming profit warning.

The next column is headed 'Yield' and shows the dividend return on the shares over the previous year. So if a share cost 100p and had a yield of 5 per cent, you would expect 5p of dividends in a year. This is not necessarily what you will receive, however. Dividends can be cut (and increased); and you may pay further tax on your dividend depending on your income.

The final column, headed P/E, shows the price-earnings ratio (for a full explanation, see Chapter 9).

A study of the figures of a particular company, Barclays, on a particular day, 11 December 1998, may help. Barclays is in the 'banks, retail' sector. A symbol following its name shows that the interim dividend has recently been increased. The share price on that day was 1283p, up 18p on the session, well down on the high for the year of 1996p but above the low of 827p. Over 4.7m shares had been traded, worth more than £60m. The shares yielded 3.8 per cent and had a price/earnings ratio of 11.8.

USING A STOCKBROKER

To buy and sell most shares you need to use a stockbroker. (The main exception is a new issue where you can apply for shares by filling in a coupon in a newspaper. Even then, you will eventually need the services of a stockbroker to sell your holding.)

Stockbroking services fall into three main categories.

Execution-only brokers will deal on your behalf but will not offer any advice on which shares to buy. The commissions they charge for buying and selling are usually lower than other brokers. A good example of an execution-only broker is Charles Schwab, the US broker which took over ShareLink.

Many execution-only brokers now operate over the Internet, which allows you to trade without ever speaking to an individual. This has lowered the costs of dealing but it has also increased the temptation to deal more often. It is worth remembering that investment is a very complex business that many professionals fail to master. If you are successful in your early trades, it is more likely to be due to luck rather than judgement.

Advisory brokers will, as their name suggests, give advice on the right shares to buy or sell; the ultimate decision still lies in your hands. Their commissions are normally higher than those of execution-only brokers, but they claim their advice and standard of service is worth it.

Discretionary brokers take complete control of your money. This type of broker is best suited to the better-off, with say £100,000 to invest, and to those who do not feel expert enough to select their own shares. Such brokers may well charge a fee, based on a percentage of the amount of money invested.

A list of brokers can be found by writing to the Association of Private Client Investment Managers and Stockbrokers (APCIMS), 5th floor, 20 Dysart Street, London EC2A 2BX.

TAX AND STOCK MARKET INVESTING

Profits from investing in shares are taxed in two ways. First the dividends earned are subject to income tax. The system is rather complicated, but higher-rate taxpayers have to deduct tax while basic-ratepayers do not.

If your shares rise in price, you may face a capital gains tax bill. The government overhauled the capital gains tax system in the March 1998 Budget. The new system, which started in April 2000, will taper the tax rate after an investor has held assets for three years. The old system of indexation for inflation has disappeared but the annual tax-free allowance (£7,500 in the 2001/02 tax year) has remained. The result may encourage long term investment but at the expense of making tax calculations fiendishly complicated.

PEPS AND ISAS

The Individual Savings Account, or ISA, is the latest government wheeze for persuading UK citizens to save more money.

Just as savers were getting used to the idea of personal equity plans, or PEPs, the government came up with a new scheme and new rules to learn, no doubt creating extra income for the legal, accountancy and regulatory professions in the process.

At least the government allowed PEP investors to retain the bulk of their old tax privileges, although only after a considerable campaign of protest. Investments in PEPs are free of income and capital gains tax.

ISAs allow a broader range of investments to be held in a tax-free form, including gilts, life insurance, national savings and long-term cash holdings. Up to £7,000 can be invested in an ISA in any tax year but this can be split three ways between cash deposits, shares and insurance-based products.

Old PEPs can continue, although they cannot receive any new money and TESSAs taken out before April 1999 can run their five year course.

UNIT AND INVESTMENT TRUSTS

Picking the right share is a difficult business. Most private investors only have enough money to buy two or three shares, and are thus very exposed to the risk of one of those companies going bust.

Unit and investment trusts (explained in Chapter 8) offer a way round this problem. They each buy a widespread portfolio of shares – private investors then acquire units, or shares, in the trusts. Those with a small sum can thus enjoy the benefits of a diversified portfolio.

It is possible to buy units in trusts which specialize in certain geographical areas (such as the US, Japan or Europe) or in commodities like gold. However, the more narrow a trust's focus, the greater the risk.

Investment trusts have shares rather than units. These shares are not directly linked to the value of the fund, but rise and fall according to supply and demand. Say there are 100m shares and the fund is worth £100m. The shares might well trade at 90p, rather than at £1. In such a case, they would stand at a discount to net assets.

If this discount narrows, the investor will make a profit even though the value of the underlying portfolio is unchanged. If the discount widens, the investor will make a loss. During the late 1980s and early 1990s, discounts narrowed across the investment trust sector, resulting in some very nice profits for investors. But when the discount widens, as it did in the mid 1990s, investors lose out.

Another development in the 1980s and 1990s was the growth in split capital investment trusts. These have different classes of shares; a typical division is for one class to receive all the income of the trust, and the other all the capital growth. These structures can be very complex and risky, and many trusts got into difficulties in the face of falling stock markets in 2001. Anyone considering buying such shares should take expert advice.

The two sectors often argue amongst themselves about which is the better. Charges are certainly higher on unit trusts; but the existence of the discount adds an extra layer of risk for those buying shares in investment trusts. Both offer savings schemes, ways of investing on a monthly basis to smooth out some of the market peaks and troughs. If an investor can find a fund with a good performance record and a low cost savings scheme, it probably does not matter whether it is a unit or investment trust.

INDEX FUNDS

One type of fund that has only become available to small investors in recent years is the index-tracker. Rather than research the market and look for attractive stocks, an index fund attempts to match the performance of a particular benchmark, such as the FTSE 100 Index.

One reason for this is lower costs. The components of an index change only rarely, so a fund manager who tracks the index faces few dealing costs. Active managers are forever turning over their portfolios in the effort to find the next winners; the costs incurred are passed to retail investors, reducing their long term returns.

The second reason is called *efficient market theory*. In essence, the theory states that all the information about a share is already included in the price. So if you notice that everyone is using mobile phones and rush out to buy shares in a mobile phone company, you will be too late; other people will have noticed first and pushed the shares up to reflect the sector's improved prospects.

The only thing that will cause a share price to move is genuine 'news' which by definition cannot be known in advance.

Efficient market theory still prompts much debate among academics and is derided by many fund managers, but the facts are that only around 20 per cent of fund managers beat the index over the long run.

Index funds will almost never be the best performers but their low costs and broad spread means that they will not be the worst. They are an attractive option for private investors.

Controlling the City

As I hope the previous chapters illustrate, the workings of the financial system are not another branch of sub-nuclear physics. They can, and should, be understood by the layman. This is not merely so that a few readers can make more money out of their savings accounts or share portfolios. It is also because the financial sector is such an extremely important part of the economy that more people ought to be able to comprehend it. This last chapter examines the question of whether the City can, and should, be controlled. There are three main schools of thought on this question.

THE FREE MARKET VIEW

The first, which might be called the *free market* view, is that financial markets work best when free from regulation. Government regulations, and particularly differential tax treatment, only introduce distortions into the market which prevent it from working efficiently. Free from restrictions, investors will lend where it is most profitable and borrowers will obtain funds from the cheapest source. Supply and demand will bring the two sides together.

It is a view which has some evidence behind it. There is little doubt, for example, that mortgage interest tax relief diverted the savings of the private sector away from the equity market (and thereby industry) and into property. Stamp tax on share transfers merely makes the London Stock Exchange less competitive than its international neighbours.

In the 1980s, the Conservatives did their best to introduce the so-called 'level playing field' system. Capital gains and income became taxable at the same rate; life assurance premiums ceased to be eligible for relief; salaried perks became taxed on much the same basis as income. In the same way, financial institutions are now treated more like equals than separate classes. Banks and building societies, for example, are now starting to resemble each other when not long ago they were completely distinct types of entity.

On the subject of fraud, the free market view is that those in the industry are best placed to deal with the fraudsters. They understand what is shady dealing and what is legitimate trading. A statutory system of control is cumbersome by comparison and results only in discouraging foreign financial institutions from doing business in London. The only people to benefit are financial rivals who will gain the income that the UK loses.

Foreign-exchange controls are also a distortion according to this view. Banks and financial institutions are not involved in a conspiracy to deprive the UK of investment or to weaken sterling. They are merely making rational investment decisions on the basis of the economic information in front of them. The best way to ensure that UK industry receives the investment it needs is to make our firms competitive and attractive to investors, not to impose controls and restrictions. If a pension fund is prevented from investing in the areas which it considers most profitable, the people who will suffer will be those who are relying on the funds to give them an adequate pension when they retire.

THE LEFT

The opposite viewpoint was traditionally held by many on the Left. One might call it the *Trojan horse* view. In essence, the Left felt that the City is in a position to frustrate the economic policies and aims of a Labour government. Until the election of Tony Blair's administration, markets tended to react fairly unfavourably to the prospect of a Labour victory. Money would flee the country, the stock market would fall; in some cases, creating a crisis very early in the life of a Labour government.

The old view was that foreign-exchange controls were essential if investment were to be properly planned, since investment abroad by pension funds is not in the long-term interests of pension contributors. If UK industry fails to receive the funds it needs, then the standard of living of all workers will fall. A higher pension will in the circumstances be small compensation.

Owners of capital frequently have different interests from the majority of their countrymen. It might prove financially advantageous, for example, to replace Wembley Stadium with a multi-storey carpark but it is likely that most Britons would oppose such a move. In the same way, closing a shipyard might bring a short-term gain to the owners but much hardship to the workers. Since it is the aim of the government, according to the old Left's view, to look after the interests of the majority, the freedom of capitalists, and thus the City, must be limited.

The fall of communism and the electoral decline of the Labour Party have left these views with very few friends in mainstream politics. Most supposedly 'left-wing' politicians now fight shy of attacking the financial sector and in many countries have liberalized their economies in the style of Thatcher and Reagan.

While the early 1990s recession showed up some of the flaws in the free market philosophy, it still seems likely to be a long time before a serious attempt is made to restrain the power of the financial markets in the UK.

A THIRD VIEW

There is, without sounding too much of a fence-sitter, a third view. While recognizing that the City is a vital part of the economy, many are dubious that it should pursue its activities untrammelled by regulation. One needs only to look at those salesmen who persuade old-age pensioners to invest in the shares of dubious companies to realize that the private investor needs protection from the sharper elements in the City. It also seems reasonable to argue that no government should stand idly back and let the City affect the economy as it will.

One particular area of concern for those who hold this third view is the short-term horizons that obsess today's fund managers. Part of the argument of this book is that financial institutions are required to convert the short-term savings of the private sector into the long-term funds needed by industry. Nowadays, however, fund managers are judged by short-term performance criteria. As a result, they tend to show little patience with companies which have long-term plans. If short-term results are not achieved, the fund managers sell their shares. This in turn leads industrial management to concentrate on short-term results as well. The result is a lack of long-term investment in industry.

This school of thought was particularly strong in the late 1980s when takeover fever ruled the US and the UK and many a long-established company was swallowed by a brash corporate raider with borrowed bucks to spend.

Many fund managers may well argue that the short-term performance criteria are imposed on them by pension-fund trustees. They in turn are under pressure from the managements of the companies whose pensions they watch over.

Reducing short-termism among investors was one rationale for some measures taken early in the life of the Blair government, notably the change in capital gains tax to reward long-term holders and the reduction in the tax privileges of dividends. Some argue the pressure to pay dividends stops industry from investing and building up their business.

The home of the free market, the US, has long used a statutory regulator, the Securities and Exchange Commission (SEC), to oversee its financial markets. Although the US banks are inclined to complain about the SEC's regulations, New York has still managed to develop as a major financial centre despite the restrictions. Obviously, this is in part due to the dominance of the US economy but it is hard to argue from the US example that a statutory system of regulation is inimical to a flourishing financial sector.

Britain has spent much of the last 15 years tinkering with its system of regulation before coming up with a new body that looks rather like the SEC, the Financial Services Authority.

The FSA formally started work at the start of December 2001. It has sweeping powers, including the ability to levy unlimited fines, and covers a broad spread of financial activity, including the power to regulate banks, which was previously held by the Bank of England. The previous system, which comprised the Securities and Investment Board, and sub-authorities covering different financial sectors, was abandoned.

The FSA has to walk a thin line between protecting the consumer from shady salesmen, and allowing business between professionals to operate without the kind of excessive regulation that might drive business offshore.

Its eight principles for a regulated firm are to: conduct its business with integrity; show due skill, care and diligence; organize and control its affairs effectively; conduct and organize its affairs with prudence; observe proper standards of market conduct; pay due regard to the interests of its customers and treat them fairly; keep faith with any customer entitled to rely on its judgement; deal with its regulators in an open and co-operative way.

That all sounds bland and unexceptionable but the devil is in the detail.

Ever since the City began, there have been fraudsters, incompetents and gullible investors. There will always be so. Ever since the City began, there have been challenges to its position from overseas. There will always be so.

But while rightly sceptical of the City's claims to special privileges and sky-high salaries, and watchful over the way financial markets constrain governments, it is hard to see any government wanting to lose the employment and income that the City brings.

Glossary

ACCEPTANCE HOUSES Institutions which specialize in accepting (guaranteeing) bills of exchange. Sometimes used as a name for the merchant banks, some of whom are members of the Accepting Houses Committee

ADR American Depositary Receipt – mechanism by which foreign shares are traded in the USA

BEARS Investors who believe that share or bond prices are likely to fall

'BIG BANG' Strictly speaking the day when minimum commissions were abolished on the Stock Exchange. Also a term used to cover the whole range of changes taking place in the City in the 1980s

BILL A short-term (three months or so) instrument which pays interest to the holder and can be traded. Some bills do not pay interest but are issued at a discount to their face value

BILL OF EXCHANGE A means of trade payment, used by companies to finance themselves. They pay a fee to an acceptance house, which accepts (guarantees) the bill. They then present the bill to a discount house, which pays them money in advance on the strength of the bill, subject to a discount on its face value. Also known as banker's acceptance and commercial bill

BOND A financial instrument which pays interest to the holder. Most bonds have a set date on which the borrower will repay the holder. Bonds are attractive to investors because they can usually be bought and sold easily

BROKERS Those who link buyers and sellers in return for a commission

BUILDING SOCIETIES Institutions whose primary function is to accept the savings of small depositors and channel them to house buyers in return for the security of a mortgage on the property

BULLS Investors who believe that share or bond prices are likely to rise

CASH RATIO The proportion of a bank's liabilities which it considers prudent to keep in the form of cash

CERTIFICATE OF DEPOSIT Short-term interest-paying security

CHAPS Clearing House Automated Payment System – an electronic system for settling accounts between the major clearing banks

CHINESE WALL A theoretical barrier within a securities firm which is designed to prevent fraud. One part of the firm may not pass on sensitive information to another if it is against a client's interest

CLEARING BANKS Banks which are part of the clearing system, which significantly reduces the number of interbank payments

COMMERCIAL BANKS Banks which receive a large proportion of their funds from small depositors

COMMITTED SAVINGS Savings made in schemes such as life-assurance policies, whereby the saver guarantees to pay a certain sum each month

COUPON The interest payment on a bond

DEBENTURE A long-term bond issued by a UK company and secured on fixed assets

DEBT CONVERTIBLE Bond which can be converted by an investor into another bond with a different interest rate or maturity

DEBT CRISIS A generic term for the problems which some Third World and East European countries had in repaying loans. The possibility of default created many dangers for Western banks

DEPRECIATION An accounting term which allows for the run-down in value of a company's assets

DEVALUATION Term, usually applied to currencies, which means simply a one-off loss in value (fall in price) of the currency concerned

DISCOUNT BROKER A broker who offers a no-frills, dealing-only service for a cheap price

DISCOUNT HOUSES Financial institutions which specialize in discounting bills. For years the channel through which the Bank of England operated to influence the financial system

DISCOUNTING The practice of issuing securities at less than their face value. Rather than receiving payment in the form of interest, the holder profits from the difference between the price of the discounted security and its face value

DISINTERMEDIATION Process whereby borrowers bypass banks and borrow directly from investment institutions

DIVIDEND A payment, representing a proportion of profits, that is made to company shareholders

ECGD Export Credit Guarantee Department – government agency which provides trade insurance for exporters

EFTPOS Electronic Funds Transfer at Point of Sale – a scheme which allows customers to pay retailers with an electronic card. The funds are automatically debited from a client's account and credited to the retailer's

ENDOWMENT MORTGAGE Mortgage linked to a life-assurance scheme. Only interest is paid during the scheme's life; when the scheme matures, it repays the capital

EQUITY The part of a company owned by its shareholders. Also used as a synonym for share

EQUITY CONVERTIBLE Bond which can be converted into the shares of the issuing company

EURIBOR Rate at which banks in the eurozone borrow from each other

EURO The new European single currency

EUROBOND A bond issued in the Euromarket

EUROCURRENCY Currency traded in the Euromarket (e.g. Eurodollar, Eurosterling)

EUROMARKET The offshore international financial market

EURONOTE A short-term security (under a year) issued in the Euromarket. Under a Euronote facility, a bank agrees to buy or to underwrite a borrower's Euronote programme for a given period of years. The facilities come under various names, like NIFs and RUFs

EXCHANGE RATE The price at which one currency can be exchanged for another

EXPECTATIONS THEORY The belief that long-term interest rates express investors' views on the likely level of future short-term interest rates. Thus if investors expect short-term interest rates to rise, they will demand a higher interest rate for investing long term

FACTORING Factors provide both a credit-collection service and short-term finance

FEDERAL RESERVE The US monetary authority which plays a role similar to that of the Bank of England

FINANCE HOUSES Institutions which specialize in funding hire-purchase agreements

FIXED COMMISSIONS Under the old Stock Exchange system, commission paid to brokers was set. This was seen as discouraging competition. Fixed commissions were abolished on 'Big Bang' day – 27 October 1986

FIXED EXCHANGE RATES Currencies with set values against each other which vary only in times of crisis when one or more currencies will revalue or devalue

FLOATING EXCHANGE RATES Currencies whose values against each other are set by market forces

FORFAITING Raising money by selling a company's invoices

FORWARD/FORWARD AGREEMENT Arrangement to lend or borrow a set sum at a date in the future for a set period at a set rate

FORWARD MARKET Market in which currencies are traded months or years ahead

FRA Forward-Rate Agreement – arrangement to fix a lender's or borrower's interest rate in advance: no capital is exchanged, only the amount by which the agreed rate differs from the eventual market rate

FRN Floating-rate note – a bond which pays an interest that varies in line with market rates

FTSE INDEX Index which tracks the share prices of 100 leading companies

FUTURES Instruments which give the buyer the right to purchase a commodity at a future date. In the financial markets they are used by those concerned about movements in interest rates, currencies and stock indices

GEARING The ratio between a company's debt and equity. See also leverage

GOLDEN HELLO Payment made to an employee of a rival firm to entice him or her to transfer. One of a whole range of City perks, including golden handcuffs and golden parachutes

GOODWILL An accounting term which describes the intangible assets of a company (e.g. brand names, the skill of the staff)

GOWER REPORT Produced in 1984, its recommendations were the basis of the new regulatory structure in the City

GILTS Bonds issued by the UK government

GROSS YIELD TO REDEMPTION The return which an investor will receive on a bond, allowing for both interest and capital growth, as a percentage of the bond's price

HEDGING The process whereby an institution buys or sells a financial instrument in order to offset the risk that the price of another financial instrument will rise or fall

IDB Inter-dealer broker. An official broker in the government securities (gilts and Treasury Bills) market

IMF International Monetary Fund – supranational organization which plays an important role in troubled economies

INTEREST A payment made in return for the use of money

INTERNATIONAL EQUITIES Worldwide market in shares. Often traded outside the Stock Exchanges

INVESTMENT TRUST Institution which invests in other firms' shares

ISSUE BY PROSPECTUS Method of selling shares in a company. The prospectus is distributed to potential investors, who are told the price at which shares will be sold

JOBBERS Under the old Stock Exchange system, those who bought and sold shares but could deal with outside investors only through the brokers

LEASING A kind of rental agreement whereby companies purchase land or equipment and pay for it by instalments

LETTER OF CREDIT A method of financing trade

LEVERAGE In speculative terms, the opportunity for a large profit at a small cost. Also a technical term for the ratio of a firm's debt to its equity

LIBID London Interbank Bid Rate – the rate at which a bank is prepared to borrow from another bank

LIBOR London Interbank Offered Rate – the rate at which a bank is prepared to lend to another bank

LIFE ASSURANCE A form of saving whereby individuals invest a small monthly premium in return for a much larger sum later on. If the saver dies during the scheme, his or her dependants receive a large sum. If the saver does not die, the sum will be paid out at the end of the policy

LIFE COMPANIES Institutions which market life assurance and insurance policies. As a group they are significant investors in British industry

LIFE INSURANCE A scheme whereby individuals pay a premium to a company which guarantees to pay their dependants a lump sum in the event of death. Differs from life assurance in that money is paid only on the death of the saver

LIFFE London International Financial Futures Exchange – exchange for trading futures and options

LIQUIDITY The ease with which a financial asset can be exchanged for goods without the holder incurring financial loss. Thus cash is very liquid, whereas a life assurance policy is not

LIQUIDITY THEORY The principle that investors will demand a greater reward for investing their money for a longer period

LLOYD'S OF LONDON The insurance market

LOAN An agreement whereby one party gives another use of money for a set period in return for the regular payment of interest. Unlike bonds, loans cannot be traded

MAKING A MARKET Buying or selling a financial instrument, no matter what market conditions are like

MARKET SEGMENTATION THEORY The belief that different parts of the debt market are separate and that therefore the yield curve will reflect the different levels of supply and demand for funds within each segment of the market

MATURITY The length of time before a loan or bond will be repaid

MEMBERS' AGENTS People who introduce names to Lloyd's

MERCHANT BANKS Banks that specialize in putting together complicated financial deals. In origin they were closely connected with the financing of trade

MINIMUM LENDING RATE Interest rate which the Bank of England will charge in its role as lender of last resort. Used by the Bank to influence the level of interest rates in the economy

MONEY-AT-CALL Money lent overnight. It can be recalled each morning

MONEY MARKET The market where short-term loans are made and short-term securities traded. 'Short-term' normally means under one year

NAMES Wealthy individuals who provide funds which back Lloyd's insurance policies. If they act as underwriters, they are known as 'working names'

NEW ISSUE The placing of a company's shares on the Stock Exchange

OFFER FOR SALE Method of making a new issue. A bank offers shares in a company to investors at a set price

OPEC Organization of Petroleum Exporting Countries – which attempts to control the price and production of oil. Had most success in the 1970s

OPTIONS Instruments which give the buyer the right, but not the obligation, to buy or sell a commodity at a certain price. In return the buyer pays a premium. Under this heading are included traded options, currency options and interest-rate options

ORDINARY SHARE The most common and also the riskiest, type of share.

Holders have the right to receive a dividend if one is paid but do not know how much that dividend will be

OVERFUNDING Tactic used by the Bank of England to influence the money supply. It issues more gilts than are needed to finance the budget deficit

OVER-THE-COUNTER MARKET Market where securities are traded outside a regular exchange

PENSION FUNDS The groups that administer pension schemes. They are significant investors in British industry

P/E RATIO Price/earnings ratio – the relationship between a company's share price and its after-tax profit divided by the number of shares

PREFERENCE SHARE Share which guarantees holders a prior claim on dividends. However, the dividend paid will normally be less than that paid to ordinary shareholders

PRINCIPAL The lump sum lent under a loan or bond

PRIVATE PLACEMENT Method of selling securities by distributing them to a few key investors

PSBR Public-sector Borrowing Requirement – the gap between the government's revenue and expenditure

PURCHASING-POWER PARITY The belief that inflationary differentials between countries are the long-run determinants of currency movements

REAL INTEREST RATE The return on an investment once the effect of inflation is taken into account

REPAYMENT MORTGAGE Mortgage on which capital and interest are gradually repaid

REPURCHASE AGREEMENT A deal in which one financial institution sells another a security and agrees to buy it back at a future date

RETAINED EARNINGS Past profits which the company has not distributed to shareholders

RIGHTS ISSUE Sale of additional shares by an existing company

SALE BY TENDER Method of making a new issue in which the price is not set and investors bid for the shares

SAVINGS RATIO The proportion of income which is saved

SCRIP ISSUE The creation of more shares in a company, which are given free to existing shareholders. Also known as a bonus issue

SEAQ Stock Exchange Automated Quotation system – on-screen service for Stock Exchange members which allows them to advertise their share prices

SECURITIES A generic form for tradable financial assets (bonds, bills, shares)

SECURITIZATION The process whereby untradable assets become tradable

SINGLE-CAPACITY SYSTEM The old way of dealing on the Stock Exchange. One group (jobbers) bought and sold shares; the other (brokers) linked jobbers with outside investors

SPOT RATE Rate at which currencies are bought and sold today

SPREAD The difference between the price at which a financial institution will buy a security and the price at which it will sell

STAGS Investors who seek to profit from new issues

STOCK EXCHANGE A market where shares and government bonds are exchanged

SWAP An agreement whereby two borrowers agree to pay interest on each other's debt. Under a currency swap they may also repay the capital

SYNDICATED LOAN A loan which several banks have clubbed together to make

TECHNICAL ANALYSTS Those who believe that future price movements can be predicted by studying the pattern of past movements

UNDERWRITE To agree, for a fee, to buy securities if they cannot be sold to other investors. In insurance, to agree to accept a risk in return for a premium

UNIT TRUST Institution which invests in shares. Investors buy units whose price falls and rises with the value of the trust's investments

WARRANTS Instruments which give the buyer the right to purchase a bond or share at a given price. Similar, in principle, to options

WHOLESALE MARKET Another name for the money markets, so called because of the large amounts which are lent and borrowed

YIELD The return on a security expressed as a proportion of its price

YIELD CURVE A diagram which shows the relationship of short-term rates to long-term ones. If long-term rates are above short-term, the curve is said to be positive or upward-sloping: if they are lower, the curve is said to be negative or inverted

ZERO COUPON BOND Bond which pays no interest but is issued at a discount to its face value

Bibliography

Margaret Allen, *A Guide to Insurance* (Pan, 1982)

Al Alletzhauser, *The House of Nomura* (Bloomsbury, 1990)

A. D. Bain, *The Control of the Money Supply*, 3rd edn (Penguin, 1980)

Lloyd Banksen and Michael Lee, *Euronotes* (Euromoney, 1985)

George G. Blakey, *The Post-War History of the London Stock Market* (Management Books 2000, 1993)

Rowan Bosworth-Davies, *Fraud in the City: Too Good to be True* (Penguin, 1988)

Bryan Burrough and John Helyar, *Barbarians at the Gate: The Fall of RJR Nabisco* (Jonathan Cape, 1990)

H. Carter and I. Partington, *Applied Economics in Banking and Finance*, 3rd edn (Oxford University Press, 1984)

William Clarke, *Inside the City*, rev. edn (Allen & Unwin, 1983)

C. J. J. Clay and B. S. Wheble, *Modern Merchant Banking*, 2nd edn, rev. by the Hon. L. H. L. Cohen (Woodhead-Faulkner, 1983)

Jerry Coakley and Laurence Harris, *The City of Capital* (Basil Blackwell, 1985)

Brinley Davies, *Business Finance and the City of London*, 2nd edn (Heinemann, 1979)

Peter Donaldson, *Guide to the British Economy*, 4th edn (Penguin, 1976)

——, *10 × Economics* (Penguin, 1982)

Paul Erdman, *Paul Erdman's Money Guide* (Sphere, 1985)

Paul Ferris, *Gentlemen of Fortune* (Weidenfeld & Nicolson, 1984)

Frederick G. Fisher III, *The Eurodollar Bond Market* (Euromoney, 1979)

——, *International Bonds* (Euromoney, 1981)

J. K. Galbraith, *Money: Whence it Came, Where it Went* (Penguin, 1976)

Bernard Gray, *Investors Chronicle Beginners Guide to Investment*, 2nd edn (Century, 1993)

Tim Handle, *The Pocket Banker* (Basil Blackwell/Economist, 1985)

Godfrey Hodgson, *Lloyd's of London: A Reputation at Risk* (Penguin, 1986)

R. B. Johnston, *The Economics of the Euromarket* (Macmillan, 1983)

William Keegan, *Mr Lawson's Gamble* (Hodder & Stoughton, 1989)

Charles P. Kindleberger, *Manias, Panics and Crashes: A History of Financial Crises*, 2nd edn (Macmillan, 1989)

Geoffrey Knott, *Understanding Financial Management* (Pan, 1985)

Anne O. Krueger, *Exchange-Rate Determination* (Cambridge University Press, 1983)

Paul Krugman, *Peddling Prosperity* (W. W. Norton, 1994)

Nigel Lawson, *The View from No. 11: Memoirs of a Tory Radical* (Corgi Books, 1993)

Harold Lever and Christopher Huhne, *Debt and Danger* (Penguin, 1985)

Peter Lynch (with John Rothschild), *Beating the Street* (Simon & Schuster, 1993)

Charles Mackay, *Extraordinary Popular Delusions and the Madness of Crowds* (John Wiley, 1996)

Robert P. McDonald, *International Syndicated Loans* (Euromoney, 1982)

Hamish McRae and Frances Cairncross, *Capital City* (Methuen, 1985)

J. Maratko and D. Stratford, *Key Developments in Personal Finance* (Basil Blackwell, 1985)

Martin Mayer, *Markets* (Simon & Schuster, 1989)

Alison Mitchell, *The New Penguin Guide to Personal Finance*, 1993/4 edn (Penguin, 1993)

Alex Murray, *101 Ways of Investing and Saving Money*, 3rd edn (Telegraph Publications, 1985)

R. H. Parker, *Understanding Company Financial Statements*, 2nd edn (Penguin, 1982)

K. V. Peasnall and C. W. R. Ward, *British Financial Markets and Institutions* (Prentice-Hall, 1985)

F. E. Perry, *The Elements of Banking*, 4th edn (Methuen, 1984)

John Plender and Paul Wallace, *The Square Mile* (Century, 1985)

Martin J. Pring, *Investment Psychology Explained* (John Wiley, 1995)

Anthony Sampson, *The Money Lenders* (Coronet, 1981)

Georges Ugeux, *Floating Rate Notes* (Euromoney, 1981)

Rudi Weisweiller, *Introduction to Foreign Exchange* (Woodhead-Faulkner, 1983)

INDEX